LITTLE CLOTHES *for* LITTLE PEOPLE

LITTLE CLOTHES
for LITTLE PEOPLE

Home-made clothes for young children age 0 – 7

Lia van Steenderen

First published in the United Kingdom in 1987 by
Exley Publications Ltd,
16 Chalk Hill, Watford, Herts WD1 4BN.

British Library Cataloguing in Publication
Data
Steenderen, Lia van
    Little clothes for little people
    1. Children's clothing
    I. Title
    646.4'06   TT635

ISBN 1-85015-074-5

Originally published in the Netherlands by Elmar Publications
© Lia van Steenderen

Drawings and cover: Lia van Steenderen

Cover design: Han Janssen

Printed and bound in Hungary

Contents

Foreword

for Carline and Doreen

In this book there are 133 designs for children's clothes which are very easy to make yourself. With just a little sewing experience, anyone can follow the step-by-step instructions. There is a complete wardrobe for babies, toddlers and small children up to the age of seven — from overalls to a bathrobe, from bib to party dress.

Making your own children's clothes is fun because you can let your imagination run wild. Sometimes making clothes is a pure necessity as well. Children grow out of their clothes so quickly that you can find yourself continuously buying clothes.
The clothes are made of practical materials like cotton, that can stand wear and tear and machine washing. For most of the styles you usually only need small pieces of material which can be brightened up by adding another material or a contrasting border. Even the ragbag is a useful object where children's clothes are concerned.
Plenty of ideas ...
For each garment there is a pattern printed to scale in three sizes. You reproduce this to actual measurements on 2 x 2″ (5 x 5cm) dressmaker's pattern paper. What you need and how to proceed, is always clearly explained. All the clothes are utterly simple; you won't come across a buttonhole or a complicated slit pocket.
The illustrator and designer of the clothes is herself a mother of two small children. As a result, she doesn't merely know what looks good but above all, she knows what's practical.

Introduction

Materials

The children's clothes in this book can be made out of almost any material. It is best to choose easily washable fabrics that don't run. If you don't like the shade of a piece of cloth, you can dye it first. Textile dyes can be bought at supermarkets and department stores. Cotton can easily be washed at quite high temperatures. This is very handy for children's clothes, which can become very soiled. Also, in warm weather cotton is pleasantly cool to wear and in cold weather, if brushed cotton is used, it is comfortably warm. Cotton material may shrink the first time it is washed. It is therefore advisable to wash new cotton material before cutting it out to fit the pattern.
Wool needs very careful washing. Wash only by hand and never in too hot or too cold water. If very frequently washed, wool may become matted or felted.

Some types of materials

BATISTE:	Fine light cotton or linen fabric like cambric.
BOUCLÉ:	Material knitted or woven from specially looped yarn which gives a curly look.
CORDUROY:	Coarse or fine ribbed cotton velvet.
CREPE:	The yarn is exceedingly twisted during weaving. It is crease-resistant.
DENIM:	Strong cotton material.
FLANNEL:	Soft woollen fabric of open texture with a light nap.
FLANNELETTE:	Brushed cotton fabric.
GABARDINE :	Smooth durable twill woven cloth.
GLAZED COTTON:	A cotton fabric covered with a layer of lacquer.
HONEYCOMB/THERMAL:	Fabric woven with a pattern of raised hexagons or squares.
JACQUARD:	Figured woven material made of cotton, linen or half-linen. Damask patterns stand out from the ground fabric with a contrasting lustre.
TICKING:	Tough linen or cotton material, usually striped.
TERRYCLOTH:	Soft, absorbent cotton fabric consisting of many tiny loops.
STRETCH TERRYCLOTH:	The same but of a finer consistency and stretchable.
VIYELLA:	Fine, soft quality half-woollen flannel.

Different materials can make very good combinations. Some examples are:
Glazed cotton lined with brushed flannel or corduroy.
Corduroy combined with shiny cotton (pockets, casing etc.)
Wool gabardine combined with shiny cotton (pockets, casing etc.)

Quilted material
It is quite easy to make your own quilted material. The outer layer and the inner layer can be made of cotton, the filling can be polyester wadding or lightweight interlining.

You can stitch straight or diagonal lines for your quilting design. You can also follow the lines of a fabric motif or applique. For transferring an applique design to fabric see the heading on page 14: applique. First baste the three pieces of cloth together and then quilt them.

You can quilt the three layers of fabric as one whole length of material first and then put the pattern on to the material and cut according to the instructions. Or, you can cut out the pattern separately from the three fabrics and quilt each pattern piece. In this case, add a very generous seam allowance of 2″ (5cm) because the material will be drawn together when it is quilted.

Sizes

If in doubt always follow the size measurement rather than the age of your child. Size is by height of the child.

HEIGHT

Size 24″ (62cm) is for about 0-3 months
size   27″ (68cm) is for about 3-6 months
size   29″ (74cm) is for about 6-9 months
size   31″ (80cm) is for about 9 months to 1 year
size   34″ (86cm) is for about 1½ years
size   36″ (92cm) is for about 2 years
size   38″ (98cm) is for about 3 years
size   40″ (104cm) is for about 4 years
size   43″ (110cm) is for about 5 years
size   45″ (116cm) is for about 6 years
size   47″ (122cm) is for about 7 years

Taking measurements

Measure over underwear. The pattern should always be a bit roomier than the measured sizes.
1. Chest width, measured over the fullest part of the chest.
2. Waist width, measured around the waist.
3. Hip width, measured across the fullest part of the buttocks.
4. Back length, from the base of the neck to the waist.
5. Sleeve length, from the shoulder to the wrist.
6. Skirt length, from the waist to any desired length.
7. Length of pants, from the waist to any desired length. (see diagram)

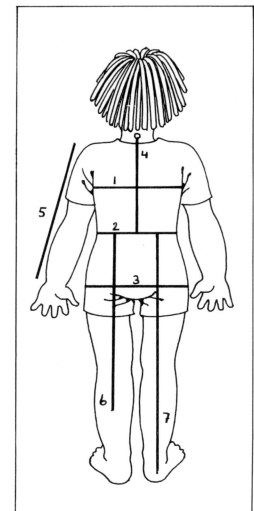

1. Chest width
2. Waist width
3. Hip width
4. Back length
5. Sleeve length
6. Skirt length
7. Length of pants

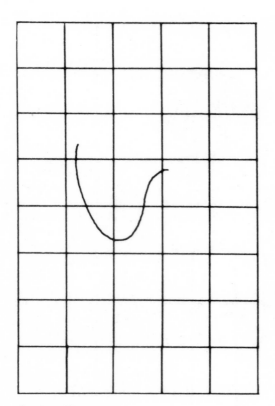
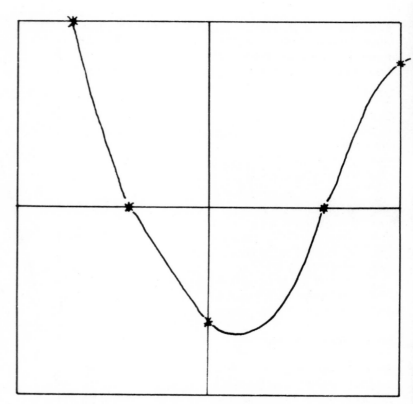

Instructions

Patterns
The patterns are drawn to scale. All the patterns can be reproduced on squared dressmaker's pattern paper 2 x 2″ (5 x 5cm) squares. You can buy this paper where you buy your fabric or you can draw 2 x 2″ (5 x 5cm) squares on a large sheet of paper.

The small squares vary in size throughout the book.

Whatever the size, each one represents 2″ (5 x 5 cm).

Mark the pattern at the points where items such as pockets, casings, loops and buttons need to be sewn on.

Reproduce the front and the back section. The section with the low neckline is always the front.

On the pattern pages, the different sizes are indicated by different lines, e.g. dotted line, solid line.

Reproducing a pattern on squared paper
Reproducing a pattern on 2 x 2″ (5 x 5cm) dressmaker's pattern paper may seem difficult to those of you who have never done it before. However, once you get started you will see that it is quite easy.
This is what to do.
Draw the longest straight line from the pattern diagram in the book on to your 2 x 2″ (5 x 5cm) squared paper. This will give you an idea of the relative proportions. From here on, mark a dot on each square of your dressmaker's pattern paper at the point where it is crossed by a line on the pattern diagram.
Having done this, you join up the dots. Watch the diagram carefully to see if the lines are straight, diagonal or curved. Don't be afraid of slight variations, it doesn't have to be absolutely accurate. (see diagram)

Laying out the pattern
When laying out the pattern, be sure that the folded fabric is perfectly flat and place the pattern pieces on the straight grain of the fabric – parallel to the selvage. The threads should run straight through the pattern piece – both lengthwise and crosswise.
Finally, don't forget the seam allowance. This should be added to the outside edge of the pattern pieces. Allowances are given for each garment.

Amount of material
The amount of material has been generously calculated for the largest size. For a smaller size you can usually count on a lesser quantity, it depends on the style. For pants you can use quite a lot less material for a smaller size.

Pinning and basting
Pin or baste a garment together first if there is any doubt about the fit. Follow the sewing instructions except that where stitching is indicated, you pin or baste.

Sewing instructions
Always read the sewing instructions through to the end before you pin the pattern to the material and cut it out. After that, follow the instructions step by step. Read each step thoroughly before you continue sewing.

Sleeves
Sleeves that are cut out in one piece with the main garment can also be cut out and sewn on separately. Just cut the sleeves off the pattern, remembering to add a seam allowance to both pieces. For example, it is fun to make sleeves out of a different fabric. The joining seam can be disguised with a contrasting band. A row of different bands looks very cheerful. (see illustration)

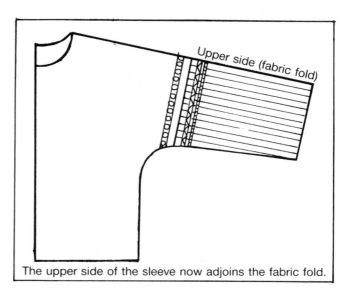

The upper side of the sleeve now adjoins the fabric fold.

Stretch fabric

Stretch fabrics should always be sewn with a synthetic thread using a gentle zig-zag stitch so that the seams can stretch with the rest of the material.

Ruched lingerie elastic

When using ruched lingerie elastic in a waistline, take a length of elastic that is 2" (5cm) less than the waist width. Stretch the elastic as you stitch the fabric, thereby giving the ruched effect.

Cuffs

Knitted cuffs to add to the bottom of sleeves or the lower edge of a jacket can be bought ready-made but you can also knit them yourself.

The cuffs should be slightly stretched while being stitched on, in order to give a puffed effect to the garment.

Bias binding

You can buy bias binding, but you can also cut the binding out of the same material as your garment or else use contrasting material. Cut the strip from the fabric on the bias – diagonally to the threads. You will often need to join several strips. Do this having the right sides together and the edges at right angles to each other. If you use the same material, you will need to buy more than indicated in the sewing instructions. Fabric that is very inclined to fray is not suitable for bias binding.

When a seam is on an inner curve, the bias binding is stitched on more tightly. On an outer curve the bias binding is stitched on somewhat more generously. This is to prevent pulling (see diagrams 1-7).

12

Diagram 1
Bias binding is first stitched on to the wrong side of the material.

Diagram 2
Then fold the binding over the material and stitch it on the right side of the material.

Diagram 3
In this diagram a loop is stitched on with the binding. The loop is on top of the material.

Diagram 4
The loop is turned outwards and when the bias binding is folded over and stitched on the right side of the material, the loop is sewn on with it.

Diagram 5
When finishing off a collar or neckline, the end of the bias binding is first turned in. For the rest see diagrams 1 and 2.

Diagram 6
The double-sewn binding hangs out like a tie ribbon. When the binding is stitched on to the right side of the material, the length that hangs out must also be stitched twice.

Diagram 7
The double stitched loose end of the binding is now folded back to form a loop, the end of which is stitched on to the back of the opening.

Pompoms
You will need: two round cardboard discs of equal size with a hole in the middle. Remnants of wool or cotton yarn.
With three or four strands at a time, wind the threads around the hole in the middle of the discs until it is completely filled in. (see diagram) Then cut the yarn between the two discs around the outer edge. Wind a double thread between the two discs around the cut yarn and tie it in a tight knot. Then remove the cardboard discs. Trim the pompom to make an even ball and hold it briefly over steam to make it extra fluffy.

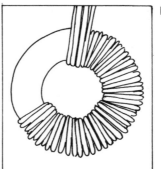

Pompoms

Curved seams

Clip the seam allowance of an inner curved seam. Cut V-shaped notches in the seam allowance of an outer curved seam (see diagram).

Finishing and flattening a seam

Lay the material flat and machine stitch ¼″ (0.5cm) away from the seam (see illustration).

Applique

Reproduce the design on 2 x 2″ (5 x 5cm) dressmaker's pattern paper. Now take the material on to which the design is to be transferred. Place a sheet of dressmaker's tracing paper (tracing carbon) over the position where the design is to be. Place the carbon side facing the material. Place your applique drawing on top of this.

Now trace the lines of the design with a pencil. The applique design is now transferred to the material. Now repeat the procedure to obtain different parts of the design on different pieces of material. Cut them out and iron very thin fusible webbing on to the backs (you can also use textile glue to attach appliques to garments).

Pin and baste the appliques in exactly the right positions on the design. Now attach them to the material using a zigzag stitch. Use closely-spaced, fairly large zigzag stitches. It is preferable not to use too thin or too thick fabrics for appliques. Also avoid stretch fabrics or velvet — these are difficult to work with. You could try first making an applique on a trial piece of fabric.

How to insert a zipper

Baste the opening for the zipper together along the seam line and press the edges flat. On the wrong side of the fabric, pin the zipper in position face down, with the teeth over the middle of the basted seam and the zipper tab ¼″ (0.5cm) from the top edge. Baste through all thicknesses and remove pins. On the right side, stitch the zipper in place using a zipper foot. Start at the top and stitch ¼″ (0.5cm) from the teeth, pivoting the fabric at the bottom corners. On an open-ended separating zipper, stitch down each side separately. Remove the basting thread.

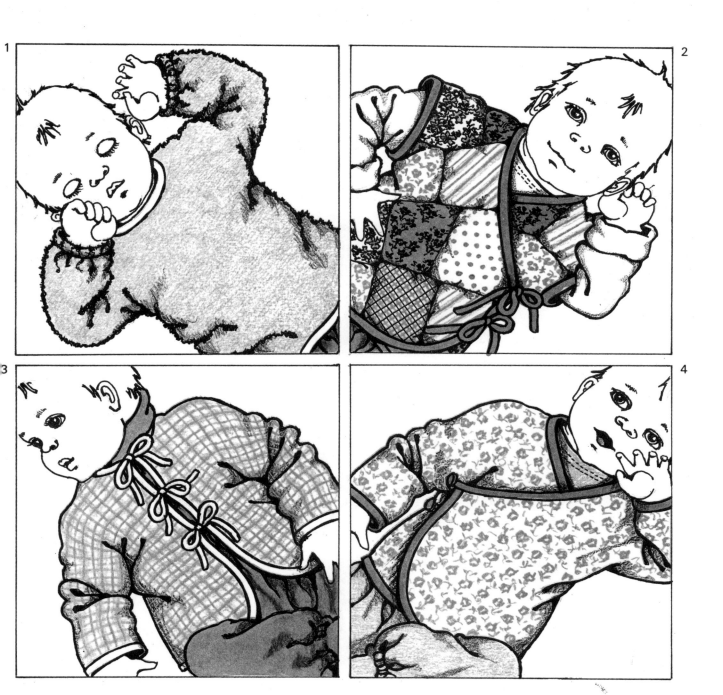

Baby tops
and jackets

Size by age: 0-3 months, 3-6 months, 6-9 months
Height of child: 24″ (62cm), 27″ (68cm), 29″ (74cm)
Materials: *Tops:* terrycloth, wool flannel, printed or plain cottons, honeycomb fabric, jersey, stretch terrycloth.
Jackets: jacquard lined with flannel, corduroy lined with honeycomb fabric, cotton lined with terrycloth, quilted fabrics

BABY TOPS   Models 1 and 7

Pattern pieces: front and back panels are cut in one piece
Fabric needed: 36″ (90cm) wide: ¾ yd (0.65m)
54″ (140cm) wide: ¾ yd (0.65m)
If seams are stitched in the upper sides of the sleeves, you will only need ½ yd (35cm) of 54″ (140cm) wide material
Notions: 2¾ yds (2.5m) bias binding,
12″ (30cm) elastic

Sewing instructions:
1 Reproduce the pattern on 2 x 2″ (5 x 5cm) dressmaker's pattern paper. Don't forget the rounded corners on the back panel, nor to plan for a seam allowance.
2 With right sides together fold the fabric in half and pin the pieces to it, with the middle of the front and middle of the back on the fabric fold.
3 Cut the side seam from the hemline to the armhole with an extra ⅝″ (1.5cm) for the seam allowance. Cut the underside of the sleeve with a seam allowance of 1″ (2.5cm). Cut the neckline and the hemline without a seam allowance.
4 Cut the back panel open down the middle fold from neckline to hemline.
5 Zigzag stitch around the edges of the pieces.

6 Stitch the side seams together. Clip the curves of the seam allowance and iron the seam allowances open.
7 Stitch the bias binding around the hemline and middle of the back. Sew on a 8″ (20cm) length of binding on each side of the back opening, 2″ (5cm) from the neckline. Fold the binding in half and stitch around the edges first.
8 Stitch bias binding around the neckline. You need a length of binding that is 16″ (40cm) longer than the neck circumference. Leave 8″ (20cm) loose on each side for tying in a bow.
9 Fold in the bottom of the sleeve. Stitch it about ⅝″ (1.5cm) from the edge. Leave a little opening so that the elastic can be inserted.
10 Insert the elastic into the sleeve and stitch both ends of the elastic together. Stitch up the opening.

BABY JACKETS   Models 3 and 6

Pattern pieces: front and back panels are cut in one piece
Fabric needed: 36″ (90cm) wide: ¾ yd (0.65m)
54″ (140cm) wide: ¾ yd (0.65m)
If seams are stitched in the upper sides of the sleeves, you will only need 14″ (0.35m) of 54″ (140cm) wide material.
Notions: 4 yds (3.5m) bias binding

Sewing instructions:
1 Reproduce the pattern on 2 x 2″ (5 x 5cm) dressmaker's pattern paper. Don't forget the rounded corners on the front panel, nor to plan for the seam allowance.
2 With right sides together, fold the fabric in half and pin the pieces to it. Place the middle of the front and middle of the back on the fold.

18

3 Cut out the side seam from hemline to underside of sleeve with an extra ⅝″ (1.5cm) for seam allowance. Cut the rest with no seam allowance.
4 Cut the front panel down the middle from hemline to neckline.
5 Zigzag stitch around the edges of the pieces.
6 Stitch together the side seams from the hemline up to the underside of the sleeves. Clip the curved parts of the seam allowance and iron the seam allowances flat.
7 Stitch the bias binding along the front and bottom edges. Stitch a 8″ (20cm) length of binding on each side of the front opening 2″ (5cm) from the neckline. If desired, repeat the procedure at 4″ (10cm) from the neckline. Fold each length in half lengthwise first and stitch around the edges.
8 Stitch binding around the neckline. You need a length of binding that is 16″ (40cm) longer than the neck circumference. Leave 8″ (20cm) loose on each side for tying in a bow.

PANTS
See the description on page 41

KIMONO-STYLE BABY JACKETS   *Models 2, 4 and 5*

Pattern pieces: front panel, back panel
Fabric needed: 36″ (90cm) wide: 1¼ yds (1.05m)
54″ (140cm) wide: ½ yd (0.35m)
Notions: 4 yds (3.75m) bias binding
For model 4: 4 buttons

Sewing instructions:
1 Reproduce the pattern on 2 x 2″ (5 x 5cm) dressmaker's pattern paper. Take note of the diffe-

rent sleeve lengths. For model 5 cut the sleeve 2″ (5cm) longer to allow for the cuff.
2 With right sides together, fold the fabric in half and pin the pattern pieces to it, with the middle of the back on the fold. Remember to plan for seam allowances.
3 Cut out the upper sleeve seamline and the lower sleeve seamline with an extra ⅝″ (1.5cm) for the seam allowance. The rest without a seam allowance.
4 Zigzag stitch around the edges of the pieces.
5 Decide which side should wrap over on top. Stitch the side and underarm seams together. At the same time stitch on loops for buttons or bias binding for ties – 2 on the inside and 2 on the outside of the other side seam. For the loops, measure the amount of binding needed for each button. Cut a length long enough for four, fold it in half and stitch around the edges. Cut into 4 pieces and form into loops. For the ties, fold the binding in half and stitch around the edges. Clip the curve of the seam allowance and press the seam allowances open.
6 Stitch the binding along the front and bottom edges. Stitch on a length (approx. 8″ (20cm)) of bias binding, 2″ (5cm) from the top of the wrapover. For model 4 stitch on a loop made of bias binding. For the loop and the tie, fold the binding in half and stitch around the edges.
7 Stitch the binding around the neckline and top of the wrapover. You will need 16″ (40cm) more bias binding than the total length of wrapover and neckline. Leave 8″ (20cm) loose on each side for tying in a bow or a shorter length if you want to make a loop.
8 Finish off the ends of the sleeves with bias binding.

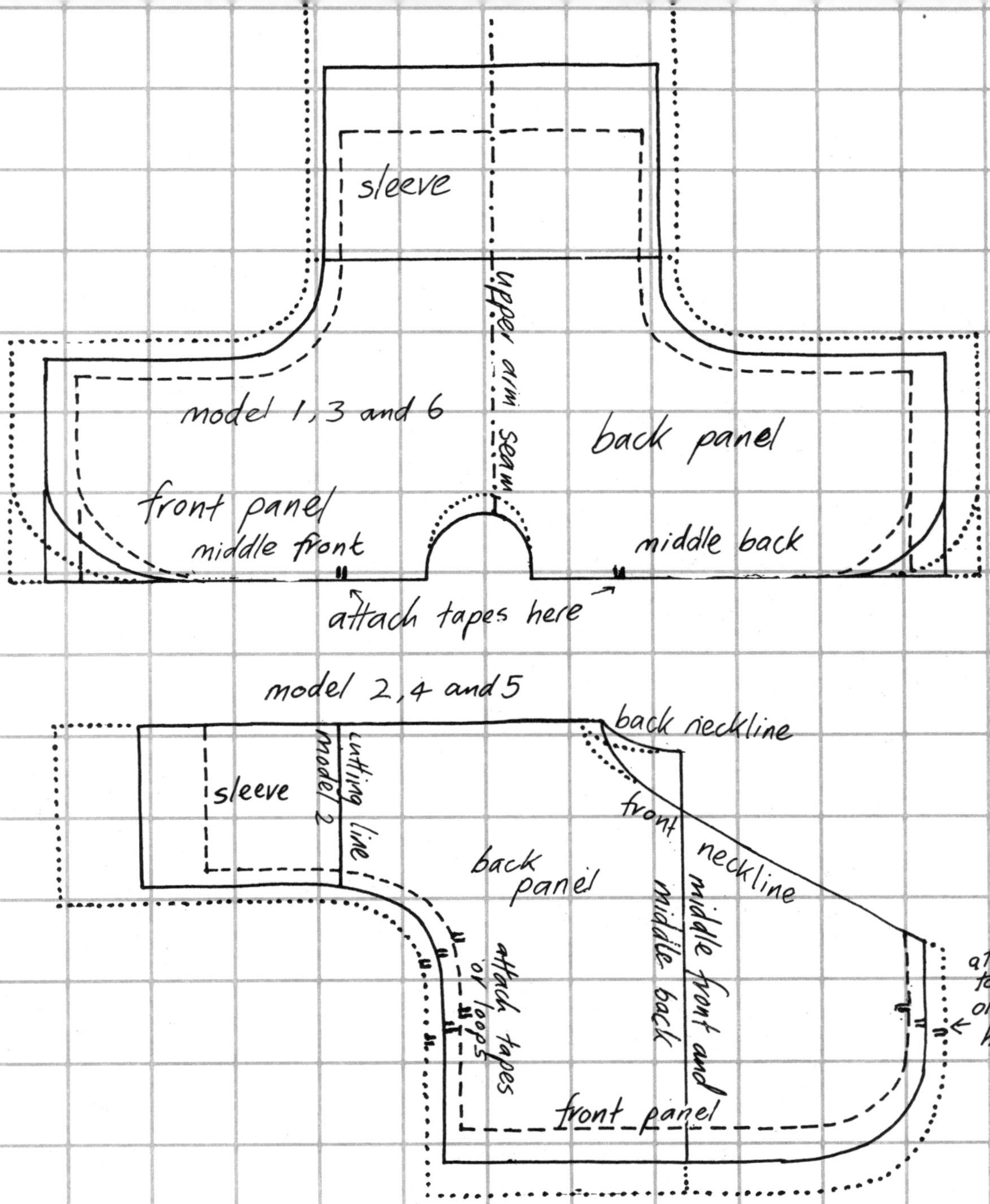

sleeve

model 1, 3 and 6

back panel

front panel

middle front

middle back

upper arm seam

attach tapes here

model 2, 4 and 5

sleeve

model 2

cutting line

back neckline

back panel

front neckline

middle front and middle back

attach tapes or loops

front panel

attach tapes or loops here

1

2

Sep 25

20

3

4

21

Stretch suits

Size by age: *0-3 months, 3-6 months, 6-9 months*
Height of child: *24″ (62cm), 27″ (68cm), 29″ (74cm)*
Materials: *Stretch fabrics like: jersey, stretch terrycloth*

Always stitch stretch fabrics with a closely spaced zig-zag stitch and use synthetic thread. The seams must be flexible.

STRETCH SUIT WITH APPLIQUE   Model 1

Pattern pieces: front panel, back panel, upper side of foot
Fabric needed: 36″ (90cm) wide: ¾ yd (0.65m)
54″ (140cm) wide: ¾ yd (0.65m)
Notions: 2½ yds (2.1m) bias binding

Sewing instructions:
1 Reproduce the pattern pieces on 2 x 2″ (5 x 5cm) dressmaker's pattern paper. Remember to plan for seam allowance.
2 With right sides together, fold the fabric in half and pin the pieces to it, with the middle of the front and middle back on the fold.
3 Cut out the front pieces and the armholes without a seam allowance. Cut out the rest with an extra ⅝″ (1.5cm) for seam allowance.
4 Zigzag around the edges of all the pieces.
5 Stitch the front foot pieces on to the front leg pieces. Clip the seam allowances and press the edges open.
6 Reproduce the drawing for the applique on 2 x 2″ (5 x 5cm) dressmaker's pattern paper. Cut the various parts out of different fabrics. Don't use very thick fabric – this is difficult to work with. Use textile glue or iron-on fusible webbing to attach the applique parts in place. Zigzag the applique on to the front panel.
7 Stitch the front and back panels together. Clip the

curves of the seam allowances and iron the edges open.
8 Stitch the bias binding around the top edges of the front and back panels.
9 Stitch bias binding around the armholes. Use a length of binding that is 24″ (60cm) longer than the armhole and leave 12″ (30cm) loose on each side of the armhole.

STRIPED STRETCH SUIT   Model 2

Pattern pieces: front panel, back panel, upper side of foot
Fabric needed: 36″ (90cm) wide: 32″ (0.80m)
54″ (140cm) wide: 32″ (0.80m)
Notions: 2 yds (1.75m) bias binding, snap fasteners

Sewing instructions:
1 Reproduce the pattern pieces on 2 x 2″ (5 x 5cm) dressmaker's pattern paper. Remember to plan for seam allowance.
2 With right sides together, fold the fabric in half and pin the pieces to it, with the middle of the front and middle of the back on the fold.
3 Cut out the armholes, shoulder straps and the top of the front and back panel without any seam allowance, the rest with an extra ⅝″ (1.5cm).
4 Zigzag around the edges of all the pieces.
5 Stitch the front foot pieces on to the front legs. Clip the seam allowances and iron the edges open.
6 Stitch the front and back panels together. Clip the curves in the seam allowances and iron the edges open.
7 Stitch bias binding along the top edge of the back panel and the shoulder straps.
8 Stitch bias binding along the top edge of the front panel and the armholes.
9 Attach snap fasteners to the front panel and the shoulder straps.

LONG-SLEEVED STRETCH SUIT   *Model 3*

Pattern pieces: front panel, back panel, upper side of foot

Fabric needed: 36″ (90cm) wide: 1½ yds (1.40 m)
54″ (140cm) wide: 1½ yds (1.40m)

Notions: ¾ yd (60cm) bias binding,
12″ (30cm) zipper

Sewing instructions:

1 Reproduce the pattern pieces on 2 x 2″ (5 x 5cm) dressmaker's pattern paper.
2 With right sides together, fold the fabric in half and pin the pieces to it, having the middle of the front on the fabric fold. Remember to plan for seam allowance.
3 Cut round the neckline without a seam allowance. Cut along the middle of the back with an extra 1″ (2.5cm) for seam allowance, the rest with a seam allowance of ⅝″ (1.5cm).
4 Zigzag around the edges of all the pieces.
5 Stitch the front foot pieces on to the front legs. Clip the seam allowances and iron the edges open.
6 Starting at the neckline, place the zipper along the middle back and mark where it ends. Stitch the back panels together below the mark. Iron the seam edges open. Insert the zipper into the opening. (See p14 for how to insert zipper.)
7 Stitch the front and back panel together. Clip the curves in the seam allowances and iron the seam edges open.
8 Stitch bias binding around the neckline. Cut the binding 16″ (40cm) longer than the neckline circumference. Leave 8″ (20cm) loose on both sides of the neck opening for tying in a bow.
9 Stitch the bottom edges of the sleeves.

SHORT-SLEEVED STRETCH SUIT   *Model 4*

Pattern pieces: front panel, back panel, upper side of foot

Fabric needed: 36″ (90cm) wide: ¾ yd (0.70m)
54″ (140cm) wide: ¾ yd (0.70m)

Notions: 1¼ yds (1.15)m bias binding,
12″ (30cm) zipper

Sewing instructions:

1 Reproduce the pattern pieces on 2 x 2″ (5 x 5cm) dressmaker's pattern paper. Remember to plan for seam allowance.
2 With right sides together, fold the fabric in half and pin the pieces to it, having the middle of the front on the fabric fold.
3 Cut round the neckline and the bottom edges of the sleeves without a seam allowance. Cut along the middle of the back with an extra 1″ (2.5cm) for seam allowance, the rest with an extra ⅝″ (1.5cm).
4 Zigzag around the edges of all the pieces.
5 Stitch the front foot pieces on to the front legs. Clip the seam allowances and iron the seam edges open.
6 See step 6 in the instructions for Model 1.
7 Starting at the neckline, place the zipper along the middle back and mark where it ends. Stitch the back panels together below the mark. Iron the seam edges open. Insert the zipper into the opening. (See p14 for how to insert zipper.)
8 Stitch the shoulder seams and iron the edges open.
9 Stitch the bias binding along the bottom edges of the sleeves.
10 Stitch the side seams and the crotch seam. Clip the curves in the seam allowance and press the seam edges open.
11 Stitch binding around the neckline. Cut the binding 16″ (40cm) longer than the circumference of the neckline. Leave 8″ (20cm) loose on each side for tying in a bow.

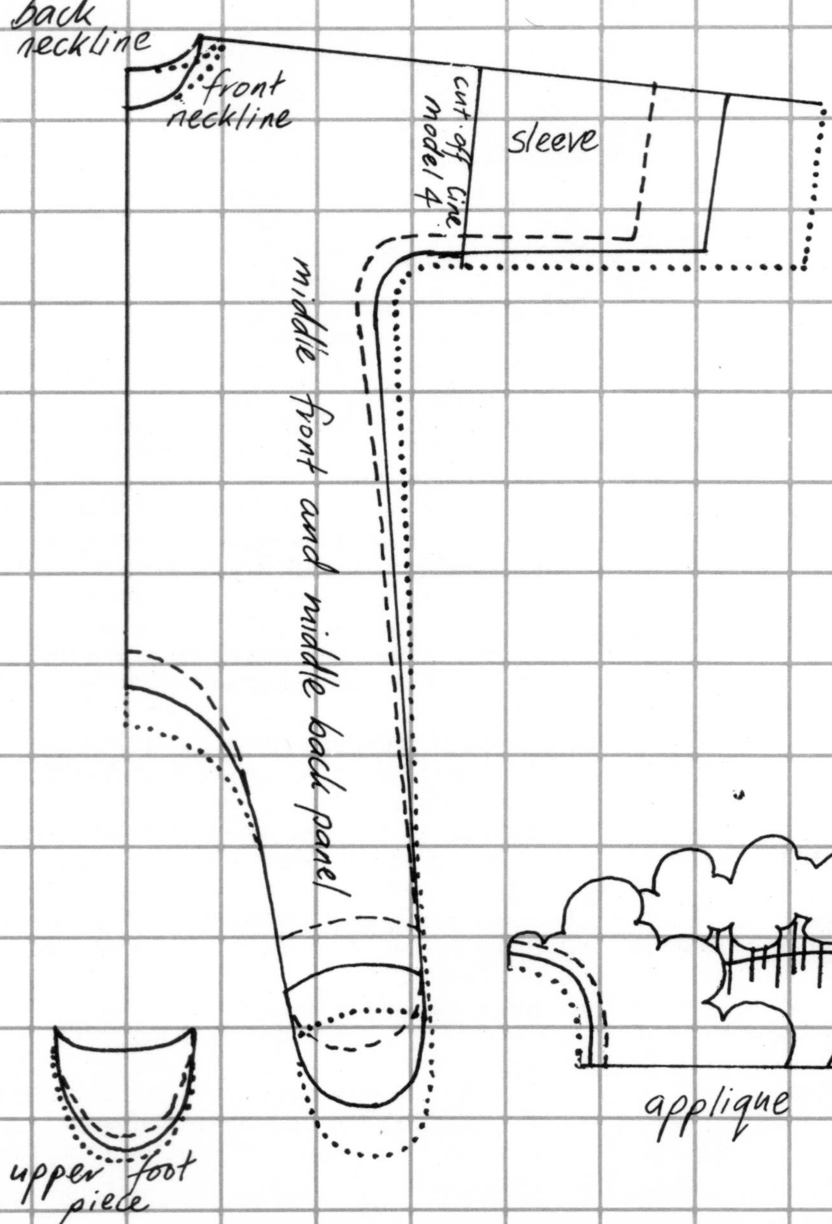

back
neckline

front
neckline

cut off line
model 4

sleeve

middle front and middle back panel

upper foot
piece

applique   model 4

24

See p 21

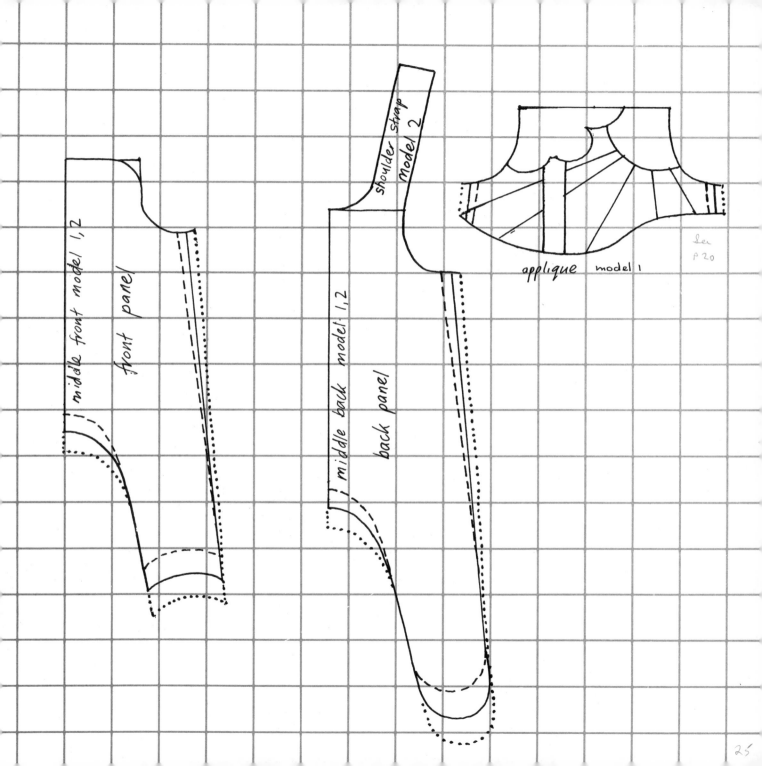

middle front model 1,2

front panel

shoulder strap
model 2

middle back model 1,2

back panel

applique model 1

25

1

26

Bathrobe with hood and sleeping sacks

28   Fabrics: *Terrycloth, flannel, velour terrycloth*

BATHROBE WITH HOOD   ~~du previ au rope~~ *Model 1*

Pattern pieces: bathrobe, hood
Fabric needed: 36″ (90cm) wide: 1½yds (1.20m)
                 54″ (140cm) wide: 1yd (0.90m)
Notions: 4½yds (4m) bias binding

Sewing instructions:

1 Reproduce the pattern pieces on 2 x 2″ (5 x 5cm) dressmaker's pattern paper.
2 With right sides together, fold the fabric in half and pin the bathrobe to it, having the middle on the fold. The hood is placed on a single thickness of fabric.
3 Cut the pieces out without a seam allowance.
4 Finish the front of the bathrobe with bias binding.
5 Place the hood on a corner of the bathrobe.
6 Stitch bias binding all around the edge of the bathrobe and at the same time stitch on the hood.

SLEEPING SACK WITH SHOULDER STRAPS
                                    Model 2

Pattern pieces: sleeping sack in duplicate
Fabric needed: 36″ (90cm) wide: ¾yds (0.70m)
                 60″ (150cm) wide: ¾yd (0.70m)
                 60″ (150cm) wide: ½ yd (0.45m)
Notions: 1½yds (1.20m) bias binding,
                 24″ (60cm), 26″ (65cm), 28″ (70cm)
                 elastic, ⅝″ (1.5cm) wide

Sewing instructions:

1 Reproduce the pattern pieces on 2 x 2″ (5 x 5cm) dressmaker's pattern paper.
2 Place the pieces on double folded fabric. With right sides together fold the fabric in half and pin the pieces to it, having both pieces against the fold.
3 Allow an extra 1½″ (4cm) for seam allowance along the top side and an extra ⅜-¾″ (1-2cm) for the remaining seams.
4 Zigzag around the edges of the pattern pieces.
5 Stitch the sides and the bottom edge together. Cut off the corners of the seam edges diagonally.
6 Fold over 1½″ (4cm) of the top edge on the inside. Stitch a line ⅜″ (1cm) from the top and then again 1¼″ (3cm) from the top. Leave an opening to insert the elastic.
7 Cut four 12″ (30cm) lengths of bias binding. Fold each one in half lengthwise and stitch around the edges.
8 Sew two tapes on to the front and two on to the back of the sleeping sack.
9 Insert the elastic in the casing. Stitch the ends together and then stitch up the opening.

hood

Bathrobe

fabric fold.

front and
back panel
sleeping sack

fabric fold

WRAPOVER SLEEPING SACK   *Model 3*

Pattern pieces: front panel, back panel
Fabric needed: 36" (90cm) wide: 3yds (2.70m)
                    56" (140cm) wide: 2yds (1.80m)
Notions: 2¼yds (1.95m) bias binding or
                    1¼yds (1.10m) cord and 1yd (85cm)
                    bias binding, 12" piece of elastic

Sewing instructions:

1 Reproduce the pattern pieces on 2 x 2" (5 x 5 cm)
   dressmaker's pattern paper. Remember to plan for
   seam allowance.
2 With right sides together fold the fabric in half and
   pin the pieces to it, having the middle of the back
   against the fabric fold.
3 Cut around the neckline and the top edge of the
   wrapover without a seam allowance. Allow an extra
   1" (2.5cm) on the bottom edge of the sleeves for
   seam allowance and an extra 1½" (4cm) along the
   bottom edge of the sleeping sack for seam allowance. Allow an extra ⅜-¾" (1-2cm) for seam allowance on the remaining seams.
4 Zigzag around the edges of the pieces.
5 Stitch the upper arm seams together and iron them
   open.
6 Stitch bias binding around the neckline and
   wrapover.
7 Decide which side should wrap over on top and
   stitch the underarm side seams together on both
   sides, stitching the wrapover in with the side seam.
   Clip the curved section of the seam allowance and
   iron the seam edges open.
8 Turn in 1" (2.5cm) along the bottom edge of the
   sleeves and stitch around ⅝" (1.5cm) from the edge.
   Leave a small opening. Insert the elastic, sew the
   ends together, and stitch up the opening.
9 Turn in 1½" (4cm) along the bottom edge of the
   sleeping sack and stitch along ¾" (2 cm) from the
   outer edge. Leave an opening to insert the cord or
   bias binding.
10 Thread the cord or bias binding through the casing.
   If using bias binding, fold in half lengthwise and stitch
   around the edges first.

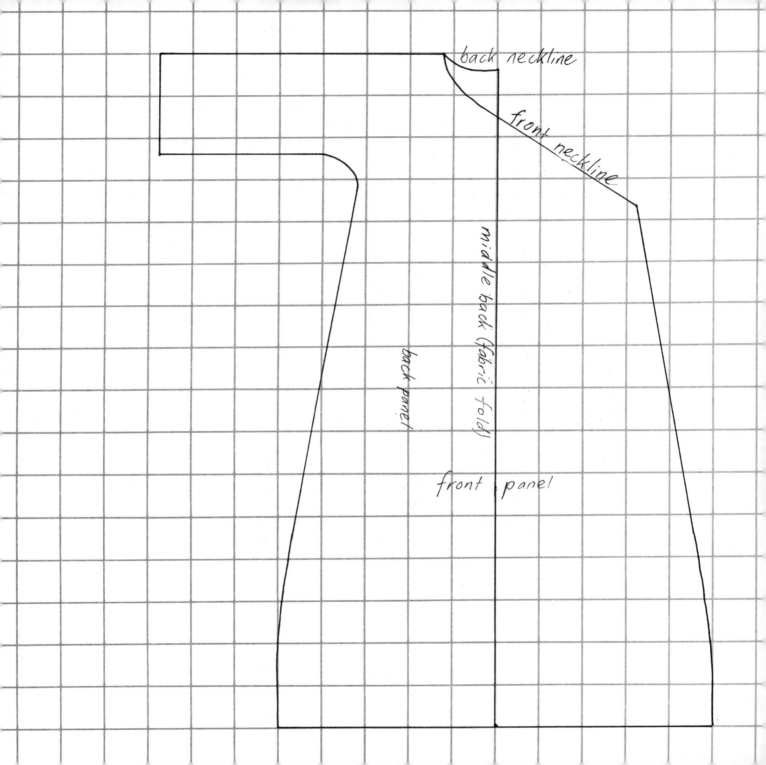

3

See P 38

Smocks and dress

Size by age: *0-3 months, 3-6 months, 6-9 months*
Height of child: *24" (62cm), 27" (68cm), 29" (74cm),*
Fabrics: *Plain or flowered cotton, flannel, ticking, velveteen, corduroy, velvet*

SMOCK WITH DECORATIVE BRAID *Model 1*

Pattern pieces: front panel, back panel, sleeve, front facing, back facing,
Fabric needed: Plain fabric:
36" (90cm) wide: ¾yd (0.65m)
54" (140cm) wide: ½yd (0.40m)
Striped fabric:
36" (90cm) and 54" (140cm) wide:
¼yd (0.15m)
Notions: ¾yd (70cm) elastic, 4 buttons, ½yd (35cm) bias binding, decorative braids

Sewing instructions:

1 Reproduce the pattern pieces on 2 x 2" (5 x 5cm) dressmaker's pattern paper. Remember to plan for seam allowance.
2 With right sides together, fold the fabric in half and pin the pieces to it, having all pieces against the fabric fold. The yokes of the front and back panels are cut out of different material. Cut out both pieces twice. The second piece is the facing.
3 Cut out the bottom edge of the sleeves with an extra 1" (2.5cm) for seam allowance. Allow an extra ¾" (2cm) on the remaining seams.
4 Zigzag around the edges of all the pieces.
5 Stitch the yoke pieces on to the lower pieces. Press the seams open.

6 Stitch the various decorative braids on to the front yoke. Do the same with the back yoke, if required.
7 With the right sides together, pin the front facing to the front yoke. Stitch along the shoulders and around the neckline. At the same time stitch two bias binding loops on to the shoulders. Measure the amount of binding needed for each button. Cut a length for two loops. Fold in half and stitch around the edges. Cut in half and form into loops. Clip the seam allowance and cut off the corners diagonally. Turn the right side out, iron the seams flat and top-stitch all around very close to the edges.
8 Repeat step 7 with the back yoke and back facing, omitting the loops.
9 Stitch the sleeve seams. Press the seams open.
10 Stitch the front and back panel together. Press the seams open.
11 Fold in the bottom edge. Stitch ¼" (0.5cm) from the edge. Stitch the various braids along the hemline of the smock. The hem can be stitched at the same time as one of the braids, if preferred.
12 Mark the middle of the sleeve hole. Place the right side of the sleeve against the right side of the armholes for the front and back panel. The shoulder seams of the front and back panel should be aligned with the mark on the middle of the sleeve. Stitch on the sleeves and press the seams open.
13 Fold in 1" (2.5cm) along the bottom edges of the sleeves and stitch them ⅝" (1.5cm) from the hemline. Leave a small opening.
14 Insert the elastic into the opening and sew the ends together. Stitch up the opening.

PANTS
See the description on page 41.

SMOCK WITH YOKE AND POCKET   *Model 2*

Pattern pieces: front panel, back panel, sleeve, pocket
Fabric needed: Plain fabric:
36" (90cm) wide: ¾yd (0.65m)
54" (140cm) wide: ½yd (0.40m)
Flowered fabric:
36" (90cm) and 54" (140cm) wide:
6" (0.15m)
Notions: 3¼yds (3m) bias binding,
14" (35cm) elastic

Sewing instructions:

1 Reproduce the pattern pieces on 2 x 2" (5 x 5cm) dressmaker's pattern paper. Remember to plan for seam allowance. On the front panel, cut the yoke out separately. Also draw the pocket on the pattern.
2 With right sides together, fold the fabric in half and pin the pieces to it, having the middle of the front, middle of the back and middle of the sleeve against the fabric fold. The yoke and the pocket are placed on flowered material.
3 The shoulder seams, the neckline, the bottom edge of the sleeves, the bottom edge of the smock and the top edge of the pocket are all cut out without seam allowance. The remaining seams are cut out with an extra ⅜-¾" (1-2cm).
4 Zigzag around the edges of all the pieces.
5 With wrong sides together stitch the yoke of the front panel to the lower piece of the front panel, so that the seam edges are on the right side.
6 Trim these edges down to ¼" (0.5cm). Sew bias binding over the top.

7 Stitch bias binding around the shoulders. At the same time sew a length of bias binding (about 6" (15cm)) on to the middle of each shoulder. First fold the binding in half and stitch around the edges.
8 Stitch bias binding around the front of the neckline. Allow 12" (30cm) more bias binding than you need and leave 6" (15cm) loose on both sides. Do the same with the back neckline.
9 Stitch bias binding along the top of the pocket.
10 Turn in and iron the seam allowance around the pocket and sew the pocket in position on the front panel.
11 Stitch the side seams and press them flat.
12 Finish off the hemline with bias binding.
13 Stitch the sleeve seams and press them flat.
14 Finish off the bottom edges of the sleeves with bias binding.
15 Mark the middle of the sleeve hole. Place the right side of the sleeve against the right side of the armholes of the front and back panel. The shoulder seams of the front and back panel must be aligned with the mark for the middle of the sleeve. Stitch sleeves to the garment and press the seams flat.

PANTS
See description page 41

36   DRESS   *Model 3*

Pattern pieces: front panel, back panel, sleeve
Fabric needed: 36″ (90cm) wide: 1yd (0.80m)
                54″ (140cm) wide: ¾yd (0.50m)
Notions: 2yds (1.75m) bias binding,
                ½yd (35cm) elastic, various strips of
                decorative braid

Sewing instructions:
1 Reproduce the pattern pieces on 2 x 2″ (5 x 5 cm) dressmaker's pattern paper. Remember to plan for seam allowance.
2 With right sides together, fold the fabric in half and pin the pieces to it, having the middle of the back against the fabric fold.
3 Cut out the neckline and the hemline of the dress without a seam allowance. Cut the bottom edge of the sleeves with an extra 1″ (2.5cm) and the remaining edges with an extra ⅜-¾″ (1-2cm) for seam allowance.
4 Zigzag around the edges of the pieces.
5 Stitch the front panel seam stopping 2¾″ (7cm) from the neckline. Press the seam open. Stitch down the edges of the opening.
6 Stitch strips of braid along the front seam.
7 Stitch the shoulder seams and press them open.
8 Stitch the side seams and press them open.
9 Stitch bias binding around the neckline. Allow 24″ (60cm) more binding than the circumference of the neckline and leave 12″ (30cm) loose on both sides of the neck opening.
10 Finish off the hemline with bias binding.
11 Stitch the sleeve seams and press them open.
12 Mark the middle of the top of sleeve. Place the right side of the sleeve against the right side of the armholes of the front and back panel. The shoulder seam must be aligned with the mark for the middle of the sleeve. Stitch the sleeves to the garment and press the seams open.
13 Fold in 1″ (2.5cm) along the bottom edge of the sleeves and stitch ⅝″ (1.5cm) from the edge. Leave a small opening for the elastic.
14 Insert the elastic and sew both ends together. Stitch up the opening.

SMOCK WITH BACK FASTENING   *Model 4*

Pattern pieces: front panel, back panel, sleeve
Fabric needed: 36″ (90cm) wide: 1yd (0.80m)
                54″ (140cm) wide: ¾yd (0.50m)
Notions: ½yd (45cm) bias binding,
                2 buttons, 1¼yd (1.0m) elastic

Sewing instructions:
1 Reproduce the pattern parts on 2 x 2″ (5 x 5 cm) dressmaker's pattern paper. Remember to plan for seam allowance.
2 With right sides together, fold the fabric in half and pin the pieces to it, having the middle of the front and sleeve against the fold.
3 Cut out the neckline without a seam allowance. Cut out the bottom edge of the smock and the sleeves with an extra 1″ (2.5cm) and the remaining edges with an extra ⅜-¾″ (1-2cm) for seam allowance.
4 Zigzag around all the edges of the pieces.
5 Stitch the middle back seam stopping 4″ (10cm) from the neckline. Turn in and stitch the edges of the opening and at the same time sew on a loop made of bias binding about halfway down the opening on one side. Press the seams open. To make the loop measure a length of binding to fit

the button. Fold it in half lengthwise, stitch around the edges and form into loop.

6 Stitch the shoulder seams and press them open.
7 Stitch the side seams and press them open.
8 Stitch bias binding around the neckline, allowing 2½″ (6cm) extra to make a loop. Make sure that the loop is on the same side as the other loop.
9 Fold in 1″ (2.5cm) along the bottom edge of the smock and stitch it ⅝″ (1.5cm) from the hemline. Leave a small opening for the elastic.
10 Insert elastic into the casing and sew the two ends of the elastic together. Stitch up the opening.
11 Stitch the sleeve seams and press them open.
12 Mark the middle of the top of sleeve. Place the right side of the sleeve against the right side of the armholes of the front and back panel. The shoulder seam must be aligned with the mark for the middle of the sleeve. Stitch the sleeves on·to the garment and press the seams open.
13 Fold in 1″ (2.5cm) along the bottom edge of the sleeves. Stitch ⅝″ (1.5cm) from the bottom edge. Leave a small opening.
14 Thread elastic through the casing and sew both ends of the elastic together. Stitch up the opening.

SMOCK WITH APPLIQUE   Model 5

Pattern pieces: front panel, back panel, sleeve, collar
Fabric needed: 36″ (90cm) wide: 1yd (0.80m)
                  54″ (140cm) wide: ¾yd (0.50m)
Notions: 11″ (28cm) zipper, scraps of material

Sewing instructions:

1 Reproduce the pattern pieces on 2 x 2″ (5 x 5 cm) dressmaker's pattern paper. Remember to plan for seam allowance.
2 With right sides together, fold the fabric in half and pin the pieces to it, having the middle of the front, sleeve and collar against the fabric fold.
3 Cut out all the pieces with an extra ⅜-¾″ (1-2cm) for seam allowance.
4 Zigzag around the edges of all the pieces.
5 Reproduce the drawing of the applique on the same squared paper. Cut out the various pieces from the scraps of material. Avoid thick fabric because this is difficult to work with. Apply fusible webbing to the back of the applique pieces. Place the applique in position on the front panel and zigzag stitch all around the edge.
6 Stitch the back seam stopping 10¼″ (26cm) from the neckline. Press the seam edges flat.
7 Stitch the shoulder seams and iron them open.
8 Stitch the side seams and iron them open.
9 Sew the bottom edge of the collar on to the neck opening. Clip the seam allowance and press the seam edges up.
10 Insert the zipper into the back seam, stopping half-way up the collar. (See p14 for how to insert zipper.) Turn in and iron the side edges of the collar. Turn in the top half of the collar. Top-stitch along the top edge of the collar. Tuck the seam edges of neckline and collar inside the overlap of the collar and sew it down.
11 Stitch the sleeve seams and press them open.
12 Mark the middle of the top of the sleeve. Place the right side of the sleeve against the right side of the armholes of the front and back panel – the shoulder seam must be aligned with the mark for the middle of the sleeve. Stitch the sleeves to the garment and press the seams open.
13 Turn in the bottom edge of the sleeves and stitch.
14 Turn in the bottom edge of the smock and stitch.

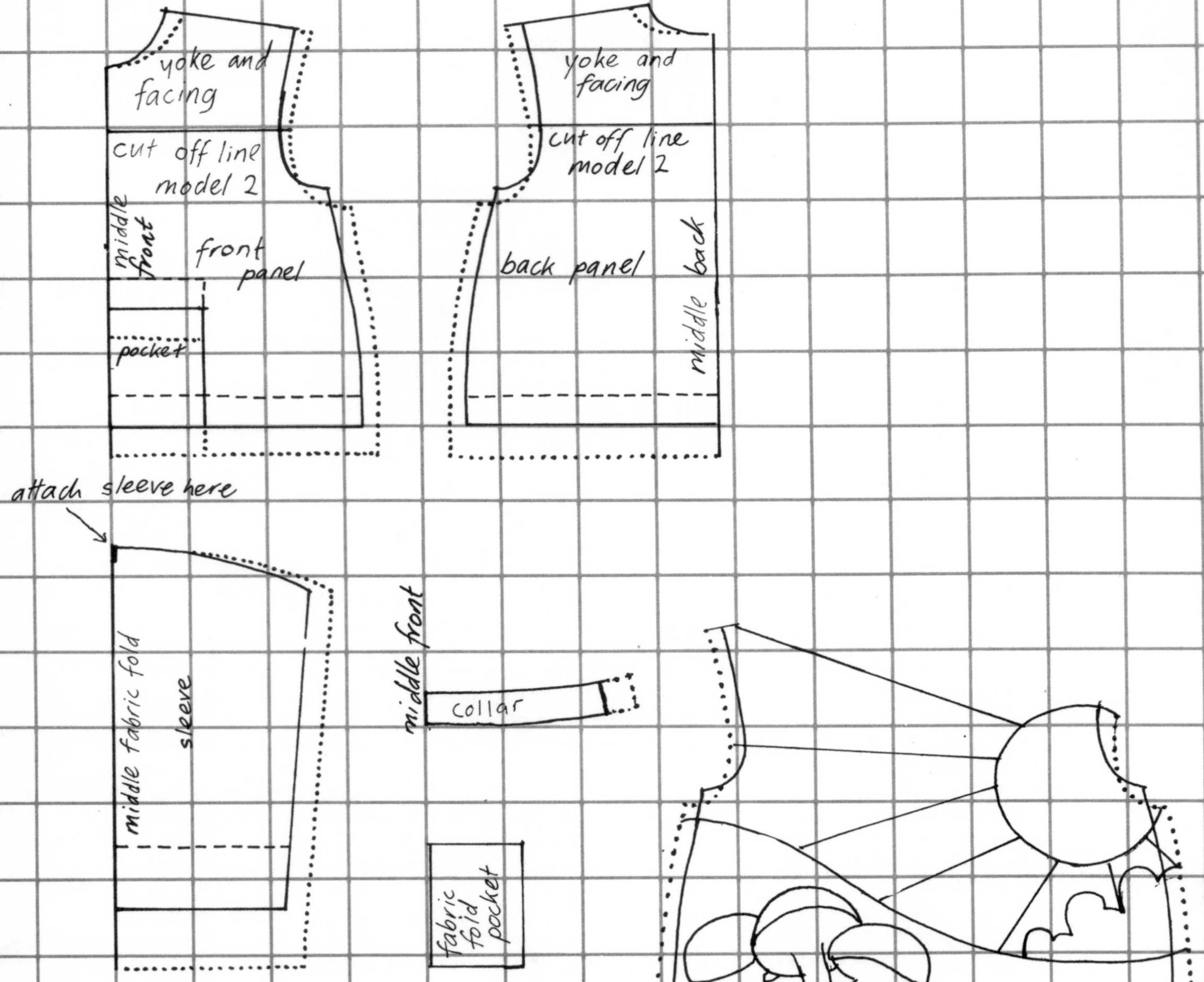

yoke and facing

cut off line model 2

middle front

front panel

pocket

yoke and facing

cut off line model 2

back panel

middle back

attach sleeve here

middle fabric fold

sleeve

middle front

Collar

fabric fold pocket

applique model 5

38

SerP 33

One-piece and two-piece suits

Size by age:	*0-3 months, 3-6 months, 6-9 months*
Height of child:	*24″ (62cm), 27″ (68cm), 29″ (74cm)*
Fabrics:	*Printed cotton, poplin, flannel, corduroy, velvet, ticking, quilted cotton, jersey.*

TOP   *Model 1*

Pattern pieces:	front panel, back panel and casing
Fabric needed:	36″ (90cm) wide: 1yd (0.90m)
	54″ (140cm) wide: 1yd (0.90m)
Notions:	4yds (3.60m) bias binding,
	½yd (35cm) elastic

Sewing instructions:

1 Reproduce the pattern pieces on 2 x 2″ (5 x 5cm) dressmaker's pattern paper. Mark the position of the casing on the front and back panel and remember to plan for seam allowance.
2 With right sides together fold the fabric in half and pin the pieces to it, having the middle of the front against the fabric fold.
3 Cut around the neckline without a seam allowance. Allow an extra 1″ (2.5cm) on the bottom edge of the sleeves for seam allowance and an extra ¾″ (2cm) on the remaining edges.
4 Zigzag around all the edges of the pieces.
5 Stitch both halves of the back panel together to 3″ (7cm) from the neckline. Press the seam open. Stitch the edges of the opening.
6 Turn in the seam allowance around the edges of the casing and iron.
7 Stitch a casing on to the front panel and a casing on to the back panel. Stitch both casings horizontally along the middle.

8 Stitch the front and back panels together. Clip the curve in the seam allowance of the underarm side seam. Press the seams open.
9 Stitch bias binding around the neckline, allowing 24″ (60cm) more bias binding than needed for the neckline. Leave 12″ (30cm) loose on each side of the opening.
10 Fold in 1″ (2.5cm) along the bottom edge of the sleeves and stitch ⅝″ (1.5cm) from the bottom edge. Leave a small opening. Insert the elastic into the opening. Stitch the two ends together and then stitch up the opening.
11 Fold in ⅝″ (1.5cm) along the bottom and stitch ¼″ (0.5cm) from the edge.
12 Take four 32″ (80cm) lengths of bias binding. Fold each length in half lengthwise and stitch around the edges. Thread them through the casings.

BAGGY PANTS

Pattern pieces:	pants front, pants back
Fabric needed:	36″ (90cm) wide: ¾yd (0.55m)
	54″ (140cm) wide: ¾yd (0.55m)
Notions:	1yd (90 cm) elastic ⅜″ (1cm) wide

Sewing instructions:

1 Reproduce the pattern pieces on 2 x 2″ (5 x 5cm) dressmaker's pattern paper.
2 With right sides together fold the fabric in half and pin the pieces to it, having the middle of the front and middle of the back against the fold.
3 Cut out with an extra 1″ (2.5cm) for the seam allowance on the top and bottom edges and an extra ⅝″ (1.5cm) on the remaining edges.
4 Zigzag around the edges of the pieces.

42

5 Stitch the side seams and press them open.
6 Stitch the crotch seams. Clip the curve in the seam allowance and press the seam open.
7 Fold in 1″ (2.5cm) along the top edge of the pants. Stitch down 5⁄8″ (1.5cm) from the top. Leave a small opening. Insert the elastic, stitch the two ends together and then stitch up the opening.
8 Fold in 1″ (2.5cm) along the bottom edge of the legs. Stitch down 5⁄8″ (1.5cm) from the bottom edge. Leave a small opening. Insert the elastic into the opening, stitch the two ends together and then stitch up the opening.

ALL-IN-ONE SUIT WITH ZIPPER   Model 2

Pattern pieces: front panel, back panel, casing
Fabric needed: 36″ (90cm) wide: 1¾yds (1.5m)
54″ (140cm) wide with a nap or a one-way design: 1¾yds (1.5m)
54″ (140cm) wide without nap or one-way design: 1yd (0.80cm)
Notions: 2½yds (2.30m) bias binding, 15″ (38cm) zipper, 32″ (80cm) elastic 3⁄8″ (.1cm) wide

Sewing instructions:
1 Reproduce the pattern pieces on 2 x 2″ (5 x 5cm) dressmaker's pattern paper. Mark the position of the casing on the front and back panels and remember to plan for the seam allowance.
2 With right sides together fold the fabric in half and pin the pieces to it, having the middle of the back and middle of the casing against the fold.
3 Cut round the neckline without a seam allowance. Allow an extra 5⁄8″ (1.5cm) for seam allowance on the middle front seam and an extra 1″ (2.5cm) on the bottom edges of the sleeves and the legs. Allow an extra 5⁄8″ (1.5cm) on the remaining edges.
4 Zigzag around the edges of all the pieces.
5 Place the two halves of the front panel together and stitch for 1½″ (3.5cm) from the bottom edge. Iron the seam open and turn in and iron the remaining seam allowance on each side. Insert the zipper into the front panel. (See instructions p14).
6 Stitch the front and back panels together. Clip the curve in the seam allowance of the underarm side seam and the crotch seam. Iron the seams open.
7 Finish the neckline with bias binding, allowing 24″ (60cm) more bias binding than the circumference of the neck. Leave 12″ (30cm) loose on each side of the neck opening.
8 Turn in and iron the seam allowance around the casing.
9 Place the casing in position on the front and back panels and stitch.
10 Fold in 1″ (2.5cm) along the bottom edge of the sleeves and stitch 5⁄8″ (1.5cm) from the bottom edge. Leave a small opening. Insert the elastic into the opening, stitch the two ends together and then stitch up the opening.
12 Take 1⅜yds (1.30m) bias binding. Fold it in half lengthwise, stitch the edges together and then thread it through the casing.

ALL-IN-ONE SUIT WITH BUTTONS   Model 3

Pattern pieces: front panel, back panel, casing
Fabric needed: 36″ (90cm) wide: 1¾yds (1.5m)
54″ (140cm) wide with a nap or a one-way design: 1¾yds (1.5m)
54″ (140cm) wide without nap or one-way design: 1yd (0.80cm)
Notions: 4½yds (4.10m) bias binding, 6 buttons

Sewing instructions:

1 Reproduce the pattern pieces on 2 x 2″ (5 x 5cm) dressmaker's pattern paper. Mark the position of the casing on the front and back panels and remember to plan for seam allowance.

2 With right sides together fold the fabric in half and pin the pieces to it, having the middle of the front and middle of the back against the fold.

3 Cut around the neckline without a seam allowance. Allow an extra 1″ (2.5cm) on the bottom edge of the sleeves and the bottom edges of the legs for seam allowance and an extra 3/8-3/4″ (1-2cm) for seam allowance on the remaining edges.

4 Zigzag around the edges of all the pieces.

5 Turn in and iron the seam allowance around the casings.

6 Stitch a casing on to the front panel and a casing on to the back panel. Stitch both casings horizontally along the middle.

7 Stitch the front and back panels together. Leave the last 3″ (8cm) open in the upper arm seams at the neckline. Clip the curves in the seam allowance of the underarm side seam and the crotch seam. Press the seams open.

8 Make loops for the buttons. Measure the amount of bias binding needed for each button. Cut a length long enough for four loops. Fold the binding in half lengthwise and stitch along the edges. Cut into four equal lengths and form into loops.

9 Top stitch along the edges of the openings. At the same time, stitch 2 loops to the front of each opening.

10 Finish the neckline with bias binding, leaving 2½″ (6cm) loose at the front on both sides for loops.

11 Sew on the buttons.

12 Fold in 1″ (2.5cm) along the bottom edges of the sleeves and stitch them down 5/8″ (1.5cm) from the bottom edge. Leave a small opening. Insert the elastic into this opening, stitch the two ends together and then stitch up the opening.

13 Fold in 1″ (2.5cm) along the bottom edge of the legs and stitch them down at 5/8″ (1.5cm) from the bottom edge. Leave a small opening. Insert the elastic into the opening. Stitch the two ends together and then stitch up the opening.

14 Take four 32″ (80cm) lengths of bias binding. Fold each one in half, stitch around the edges and thread them through the casings.

SLEEVELESS SUIT   *Model 4*

Pattern pieces: front panel, back panel, casing
Fabric needed: 36″ (90cm) wide: 1yd (0.90 m)
                   54″ (140cm) wide: ¾yd (0.75 m)
Notions: 7yds (6.40 m) bias binding,
                   ½yd (40cm) elastic 3/8″ (1cm) wide

Sewing instructions:

1 Reproduce the pattern pieces on 2 x 2″ (5 x 5cm) dressmaker's pattern paper. Mark the position of the casing on the front and back panels and remember to plan for the seam allowance.

2 With right sides together fold the fabric in half and pin the pattern pieces to it, having the middle of the front and middle of the back against the fold.

3 Cut out the neckline, shoulder seams and armholes without a seam allowance. Allow an extra 1″ (2.5cm) on the bottom edge of the legs for seam allowance and an extra 3/8-3/4″ (1-2cm) on the remaining edges.

4 Zigzag around the edges of all the pieces.
5 Turn in and iron the seam allowance of the casings.
6 Stitch a casing on to the front panel and a casing on to the back panel. Stitch both casings horizontally along the middle.
7 Stitch the front and back panels together.
8 Clip the curves in the seam allowance of the underarm side seam and the crotch seam. Iron the seams open.
9 Finish shoulders and armholes with bias binding. At the same time, stitch 8" (20cm) lengths of bias binding on where indicated.
10 Finish the front and back neckline with bias binding. For both the front and the back, take 16" (40cm) more bias binding than the neckline width and leave 8" (20cm) loose on each side.
11 Turn in 1" (2.5cm) along the bottom edge of the legs and stitch ⅝" (1.5cm) from the bottom edge. Leave a small opening. Insert the elastic into the opening, stitch the two ends together and then stitch up the opening.
12 Take four 32" (80cm) lengths of bias binding. Fold each length in half, stitch along both edges and then thread them through the casings.

TOP *Model 5*

Pattern pieces: front panel, back panel
Fabric needed: 36" (90cm) wide: 1yd (0.90 m)
54" (140cm) wide: 1yd (0.90 m)
Notions: ¾yd (60cm) bias binding,
1½yd (1.35m) elastic ⅜" (1cm) wide,
2 buttons

Sewing instructions:

1 Reproduce the pattern pieces on 2 x 2" (5 x 5cm) dressmaker's pattern paper.
2 With right sides together fold the fabric in half and pin the pattern pieces to it, having the middle of the front against the fabric fold.
3 Cut out the neckline without a seam allowance. Allow an extra 1" (2.5cm) along the bottom edge of the sleeves and an extra 1½" (4cm) along the bottom edge of the front and back for seam allowance. Allow an extra ⅜-¾" (1-2cm) on the remaining edges.
4 Zigzag around the edges of the pieces.
5 Stitch the two halves of the back panel together, stopping 4" (10cm) from the neckline. Press the seam open. Stitch along the edges of the opening. At the same time stitch on a loop made from bias binding, halfway up one side of the opening. To make the loop, cut a length of bias binding to go around the button. Fold it in half lengthwise and stitch around the edges. Form into loop.
6 Stitch the front and the back panel together. On one side seam leave the 1½" (4cm) hemline seam allowance open. Clip the curves in the underarm side seam allowances. Press the seams open.
7 Finish the neckline with bias binding. On one side leave 2½" (6cm) loose to make a loop. Make sure that it is on the same side as the other loop.
8 Sew on the buttons opposite the loops.
9 Turn in 1" (2.5cm) along the bottom edge of the sleeves and stitch ⅝" (1.5cm) from the bottom edge. Leave a small opening. Insert the elastic. Stitch the two ends together and then stitch up the opening.

10 Turn in 1½″ (4cm) along the bottom edge of the jacket and stitch down ⅝″ (1.5cm) from the bottom edge. Stitch down once again 1¼″ (3cm) from the bottom edge. Thread elastic through both casings and stitch the ends together.

BAGGY PANTS

See the instructions for model 1.

ALL-IN-ONE SUIT WITH BOWS   *Model 6*

Pattern pieces: front panel, back panel
Fabric needed: 36″ (90cm) wide: 1¾yds (1.5m)
54″ (140cm) wide for material with a nap or one-way design: 1⅝yds (1.50m)
54″ (140cm) wide for material without nap or one-way design: 32″ (0.80m)
Notions: 3yds (2.80m) bias binding, 32″ (80cm) elastic ⅜″ (1cm) wide

Sewing instructions:

1 Reproduce the pattern pieces on 2 x 2″ (5 x 5cm) dressmaker's pattern paper. Remember to plan for seam allowance.
2 With right sides together fold the fabric in half and pin the pieces to it, having the middle of the front and middle of the back against the fold.
3 Cut out the neckline without a seam allowance. Allow an extra 1″ (2.5cm) on the bottom edge of the sleeves and the legs for seam allowance, and an extra ⅜-¾″ (1-2cm) on the remaining edges.
4 Zigzag around the edges of the pieces.
5 Stitch the front and back panels together, leaving the last 2¾″ (7cm) open in both upper arm seams.

Clip the curves of the seam allowance in the underarm side seams and the crotch seam and press the seams open.

6 To make the tapes, take 64″ (160cm) of bias binding and fold in half lengthwise. Stitch along both edges and then cut into eight 8″ (20cm) lengths.
7 Stitch along the edges of the openings. At the same time, stitch on the 8″ (20cm) tapes of bias binding where indicated on pattern.
8 Finish the front and back necklines with bias binding. Allow 16″ (40cm) more binding than the neck width on both the front and the back. Leave 8″ (20cm) loose at each end for bows.
9 Turn in 1″ (2.5cm) along the bottom edge of the sleeves and stitch down ⅝″ (1.5cm) from the bottom edge. Leave a small opening. Thread elastic through the casing, stitch the ends together and then stitch up the opening.
10 Turn in 1″ (2.5cm) along the bottom edge of the legs. Stitch ⅝″ (1.5cm) from the bottom edge. Leave a small opening. Insert the elastic and thread it through the casing. Stitch the ends together and then stitch up the opening.

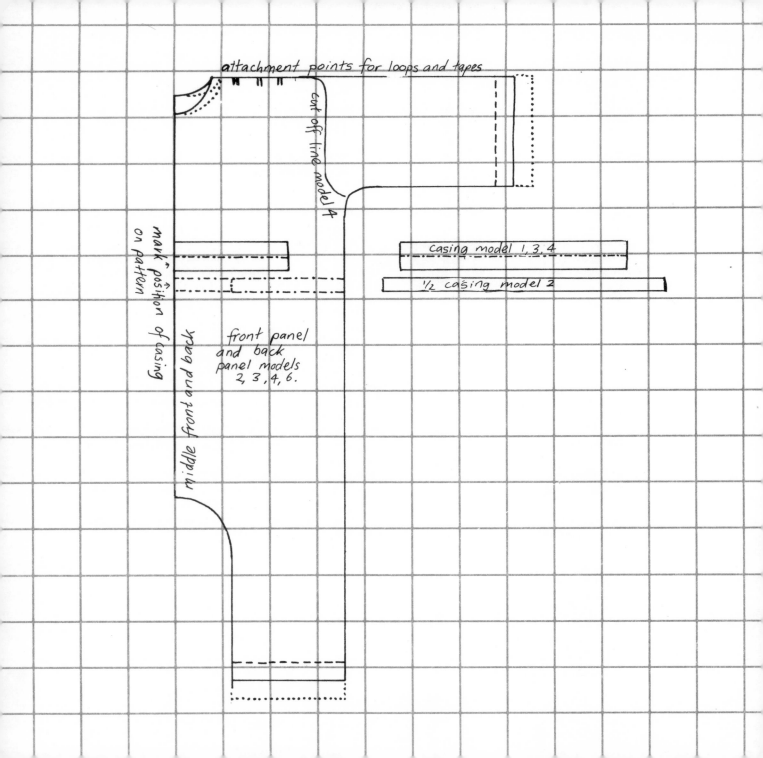

attachment points for loops and tapes

cut off line model 4

mark position of casing on pattern

middle front and back

front panel
and back
panel models
2, 3, 4, 6.

casing model 1, 3, 4

½ casing model 2

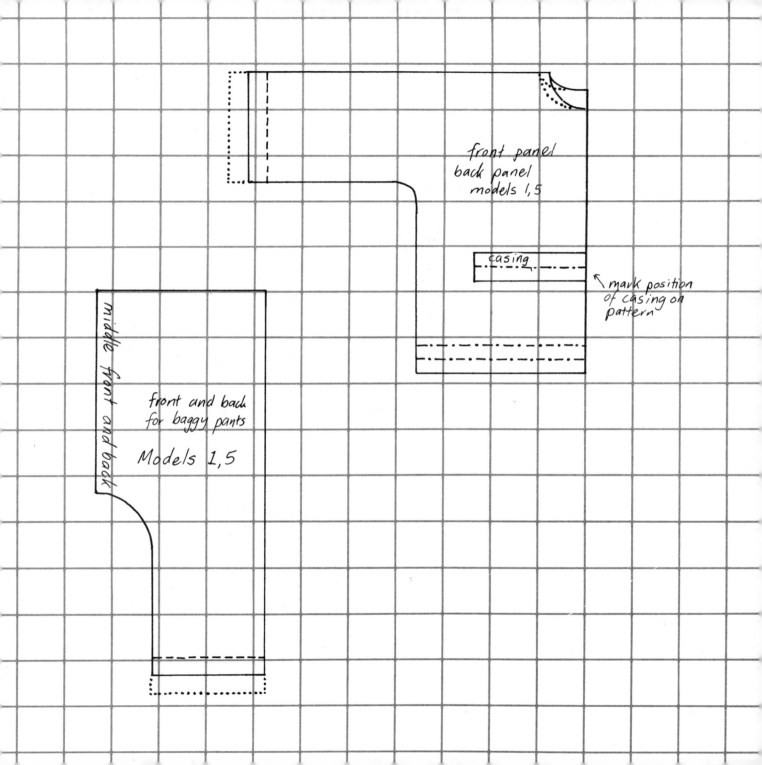

front panel
back panel
models 1, 5

casing

← mark position
of casing on
pattern

middle front and back

front and back
for baggy pants

Models 1, 5

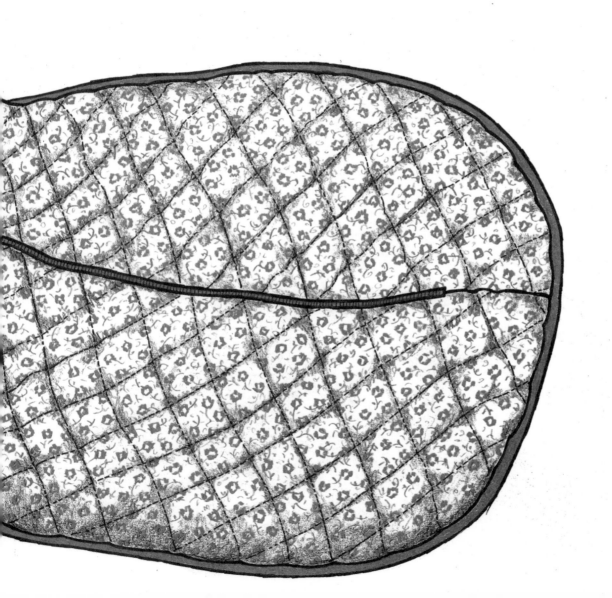

2

Sleeping sack for children aged 6 months-2 years, quilt and cover for cradle and crib

Fabrics: *quilted cotton, flannel, cotton lined with flannel.*

SLEEPING SACK Model 1

Pattern pieces: front panel, back panel
Fabric needed: 36" (90cm) wide: 2yds (1.90m)
54" (140cm) wide: 1⅛yds (1.0m)
the pattern pieces are laid out the opposite way to each other

Notions: 30" (75cm) zipper, 4yds (3.80m) bias binding. If using quilted fabric or double thickness fabric, use extra wide binding as it is easier to work with.

Sewing instructions:

1 Reproduce the pattern pieces on 2 x 2" (5 x 5cm) dressmaker's pattern paper. Remember to plan for seam allowance.
2 With right sides together fold the fabric in half and pin the pieces to it, having the middle back seam on the fabric fold.
3 Cut out the middle front panel with an extra ¾" (2cm) for seam allowance. Allow an extra ⅜-¾" (1-2cm) on shoulder seams for seam allowance and cut out the remaining edges without a seam allowance.
4 Zigzag around the edges of the pieces.
5 With the right sides of the front panels together and starting at the top edge, place the zipper along the middle front seam line. Mark the fabric where the zipper finishes and stitch the middle front seam

from the mark to the bottom edge. Insert the zipper into the middle front opening. (See p14 for how to insert zipper.)
6 Stitch the shoulder seams and press them open.
7 Finish the edges of the sleeves with bias binding.
8 Finish the neckline with bias binding. Allow an extra 16" (40cm) more bias binding than you need for the neckline and leave 8" (20cm) loose on both sides.
9 Using bias binding, stitch the front and the back panels together all the way around.

PATCHWORK QUILT Model 2

Fabric needed: *For the cradle quilt:*
54" (140cm) wide thick flannel or wadding: ⅞yd (0.84m)
54" (140cm) wide cotton: ⅞yd (0.84m)
For the crib quilt:
54" (140cm) wide thick flannel or wadding: 1½yds (1.40m)
54"(140cm)wide cotton: 1½yds(1.40m)
All sorts of cotton scraps for the patchwork cover

Notions: 4yds (3.50m) extra wide bias binding for the cradle quilt
5¼yds (4.80m) extra wide bias binding for the crib quilt

Sewing instructions:

1 Cut out 36 squares measuring 6¼" x 6¼" (16 x 16cm) for a cradle quilt.
Cut out 35 squares measuring 8½" x 8½" (22 x 22cm) for a crib quilt.
2 Zigzag around the edges of all the squares.

3 To make strips, stitch the squares together, leaving a ⅜″ (1cm) seam edge. Iron the edges open. Stitch the strips together, again leaving a ⅜″ (1cm) seam edge. Iron the edges open.
4 Take a piece of wadding or flannel the same size as the patchwork cover.
5 Take a piece of cotton the same size as the patch-work cover.
6 Place the three layers on top of each other. The layer of flannel or wadding is placed in between the other two layers and the three layers are subsequently stitched all around the edges with extra wide bias binding.

QUILT COVER   *Model 2*

Fabric needed: *For a cradle quilt cover:*
54″ (140cm) wide cotton: 1yd (0.90m)
For a crib quilt cover:
54″ (140cm) wide cotton: 1½yds (1.40m)
For the bottom layer, all sorts of cotton scraps
Notions: 32″ (80cm) bias binding or snap fasteners

Sewing instructions:
1 Cut out 36 squares measuring 6¼″ x 6¼″ (16 x 16cm) for a cradle quilt cover.
Cut out 35 squares measuring 8½″ x 8½″ (22 x 22cm) for a crib quilt cover.
2 Zigzag around the edges of each square.
3 To make strips, stitch the squares together, leaving a ⅜″ (1cm) seam edge. Press the edges open. Stitch the strips together, again leaving a ⅜″ (1cm) seam edge. Iron the edges open.

4 Take a piece of cotton fabric the same size as the patchwork layer or make another patchwork layer. Zigzag around the edge of the fabric. Stitch the two layers of fabric together on three sides.
5 Turn in ⅜″ (1cm) along the bottom edge and stitch it down.
6 To fasten the opening, either make tapes from bias binding and attach these to both sides of the opening or use snap fasteners.

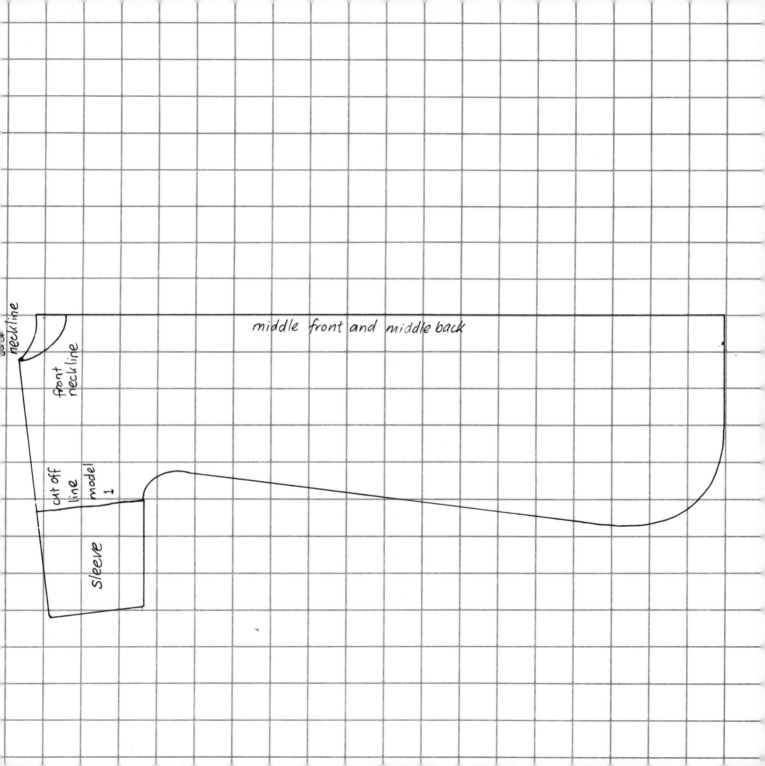

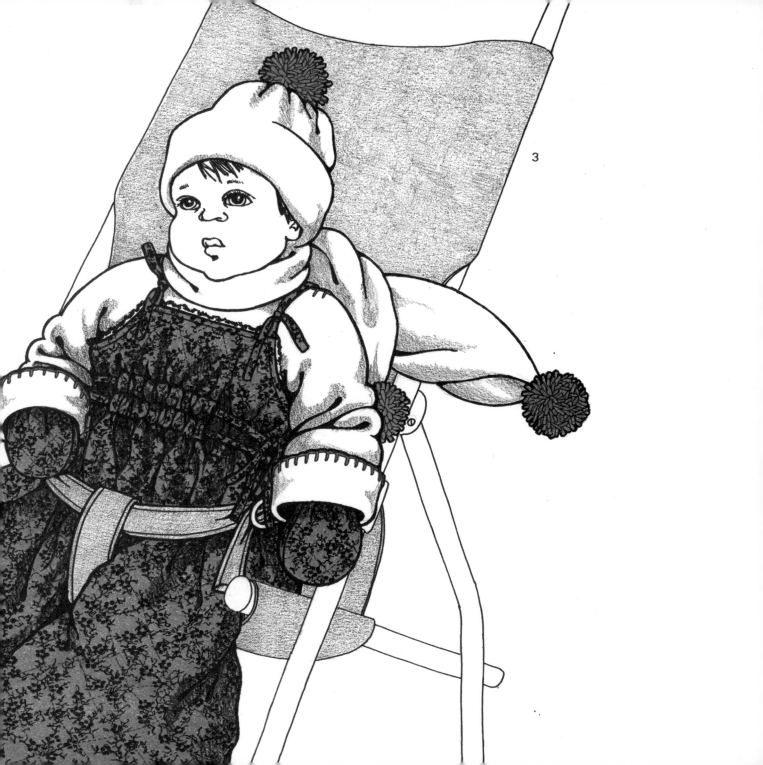

3

Toddlers playsuits
for indoors and outdoors

Size by age: *0-3mths, 3-6mths, 6-9mths, 9mths-1yr*
Height of child: *24" (62cm), 27" (68cm), 29" (74cm), 32" (80cm)*
Fabrics: *Plain cotton, printed cotton, flannel, corduroy, velvet, ticking, twill, quilted cotton.*

PLAYSUIT WITH SHOULDER TIES　　　Model 1

Pattern pieces: front panel, back panel, front facing, back facing, casing, short band, long band
Fabric needed: 36" (90cm) wide: 1¼yds (1.15m)
54" (140cm) wide: 1⅛yds (0.95m)
Notions: ½yd (45cm) elastic ⅜" (1cm) wide

Sewing instructions:

1 Reproduce the pattern pieces on 2 x 2" (5 x 5cm) dressmaker's pattern paper. Also reproduce the facing for the front and back panel. Remember to plan for seam allowance. Mark the position of the casings on the front and back panels.
2 With right sides together fold the fabric in half and pin the front panel, back panel and the two facings to it, having the middle front and middle back seams against the fabric fold. Then pin the casing and bands to the fabric, having the bands horizontal. Cut out the bands four times.
3 Cut the bottom edges of the legs with an extra 1" (2.5cm) for seam allowance. Allow an extra ⅜-¾" (1-2cm) on the remaining edges.
4 Zigzag around the edges of the pieces.
5 Turn in and iron the seam allowance of each band and then fold the bands in half lengthwise and press. Now stitch them all around the edges.

6 With the raw edges together, place the short bands where indicated on the right side of the front and back panels so that they are hanging down from the panel. Baste the bands in position.
7 With right sides together, stitch the top edge of the front and the back facings to the front and back panels. (The shoulder bands are stitched on at the same time.)
8 Stitch the front and back panels together. Also the side seams of the front and back facing. Clip the curves in the seam allowance of the crotch seam and press the seams open.
9 Turn the facing in and top-stitch all the way around the edge on the right side.
10 Turn in and iron the seam allowance of the casings. Stitch the casings where indicated on the front and the back panel. Stitch horizontally along the middle of the casings. Thread the long bands through the casings.
11 Turn in 1" (2.5cm) along the bottom edge of the legs and stitch them ⅝" (1.5cm) from the bottom edge. Leave a small opening. Insert elastic into the opening, stitch the ends together and then stitch up the opening.

STRIPED PLAYSUIT　　　Model 2

Pattern pieces: front panel, back panel, front facing, back facing, short band
Fabric needed: 36" (90cm) wide: 1yd (0.90m)
54" (140cm) wide: ¾yd (0.70m)
Notions: 2¼yds (2m) elastic ⅜" (1cm) wide

Sewing instructions:

Follow the instructions for model 1. The only variations are steps 2, 8 and 10.

2 See model 1, omitting the long bands and the casing.

8 Stitch the sides of the front and back panels together. Start on one side with the side seam of the front and back facings. On the other side leave part of the facing side seam open for the elastic. Stitch the crotch seam and clip the curve of the seam allowance. Press the seams open.

10 To make the casings, do four rows of stitching around the garment, as indicated on the pattern, leaving ⅝″ (1.5cm) between each row. In doing so, the facings are stitched to the front and back panels. Insert elastic into the casings through the openings in the facing side seam, stitch the ends of the elastic together and stitch up the openings.

PLAYSUIT FOR OUTDOORS　　　　*Model 3*

Pattern pieces: front panel, back panel, front facing, back facing, casing, short band, long band
Fabric needed: 36″ (90cm) wide: 1⅜yd (1.25m)
　　　　　　　　54″ (140cm) wide: 1⅛yd (1.05m)

Sewing instructions:

Follow the instructions for model 1. There is a change in step 8 and step 11 is omitted.

8 Stitch the front and back panels together. Also stitch the sides of the front and back facing. Clip all the curves in the seam edges and press the seams open.

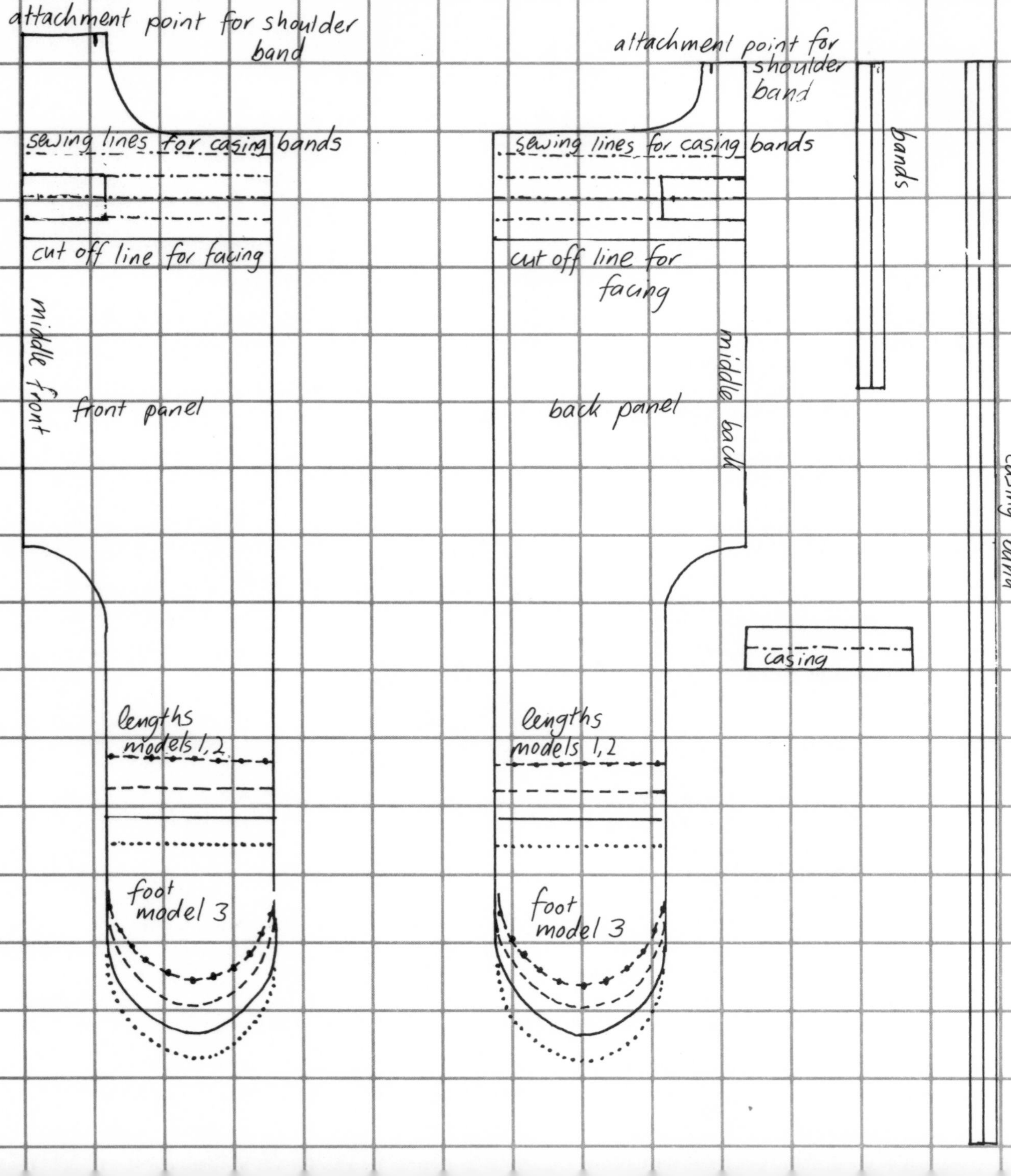

attachment point for shoulder band

attachment point for shoulder band

sewing lines for casing bands

sewing lines for casing bands

cut off line for facing

cut off line for facing

middle front

middle back

front panel

back panel

bands

casing band

casing

lengths models 1,2

lengths models 1,2

foot model 3

foot model 3

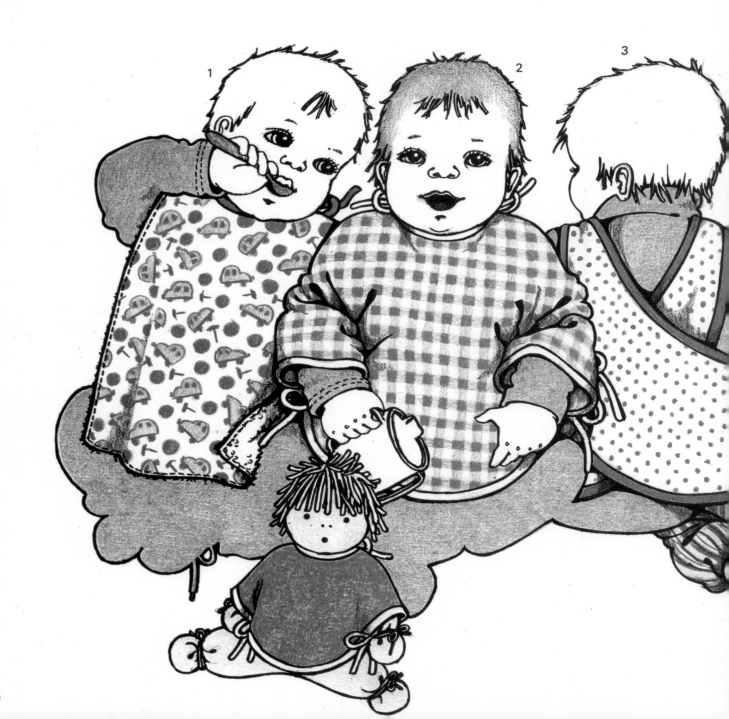

4 5 6

61

All sorts of bibs

Fabrics: *Terrycloth, flannelette.*
Cotton lined with terrycloth, cotton lined with flannelette, quilted fabric.

SQUARE BIB   Model 1

Fabric needed: 36" (90cm) wide: ⅝yd (0.55m)
54" (140cm) wide: ⅝yd (0.55m)

Notions: 1⅛yds (1m) bias binding

Sewing instructions:

1 Reproduce the bib on 2 x 2" (5 x 5cm) dressmaker's pattern paper. Remember to plan for seam allowance.
2 With right sides together fold the fabric in half and pin the pattern to it, having the middle of the front against the fabric fold.
3 Cut out the pattern once in smooth cotton fabric and once in terrycloth. Cut out the neckline without a seam allowance. Allow an extra ⅜-¾" (1-2cm) for seam allowance around all the other edges.
4 Zigzag around the edges of the bib.
5 With right sides together, stitch the two pieces together leaving an opening on one edge.
6 Cut off the corners diagonally.
7 Turn the bib right side out and press.
8 Top-stitch around the bib, keeping close to the edge.
9 Finish the neckline with bias binding. Allow 24" (60cm) more bias binding than you need for the neckline and leave 12" (30cm) loose on each side.

BIB WITH SLEEVES   Model 2

Fabric needed: 36" (90cm) wide: 1yd (0.90m)
54" (140cm) wide: 1yd (0.90m)
If the pattern is laid out across the fabric: 36" (90cm) wide: ⅝yd (0.50m)
54" (140cm) wide: ⅝yd (0.50m)

Notions: 4½yds (4.20m) bias binding

Sewing instructions:

1 Reproduce the bib on 2 x 2" (5 x 5cm) dressmaker's pattern paper.
2 With right sides together fold the fabric in half and pin the pattern to it, having the middle of the front against the fabric fold.
3 Cut out the bib without a seam allowance, with the exception of the middle back which has a seam allowance of ⅜" (1cm). This is achieved by cutting out the middle of the back along the fabric fold.
4 Zigzag around the edges of the bib.
5 Turn in the middle back seam allowance and stitch down ¼" (0.5cm) from the edge.
6 To make ties, take four 12" (30cm) lengths of bias binding. Fold each one in half lengthwise and stitch around the edges. Place ties where indicated on the pattern and baste.
7 Stitch bias binding around the edge of the bib, starting and finishing at the middle of the back. The ties will be stitched on at the same time.
8 Finish the neckline with bias binding. Allow 24" (60cm) more bias binding than you need for the neckline and leave 12" (30cm) loose on each side.

WRAP-AROUND BIB

Model 3

Fabric needed: 36″ (90cm) wide: ⅝yd (0.50m)
54″ (140cm) wide: ⅝yd (0.50m)
Notions: 3¼yds (3m) bias binding,
2 snap fasteners

Sewing instructions:

1 Reproduce the bib on 2 x 2″ (5 x 5cm) dressmaker's pattern paper.
2 With right sides together fold the fabric in half and pin the bib to it, having the middle of the front against the fabric fold. Cut out the pattern without a seam allowance.
3 Finish all the way around the edge of the bib with bias binding.
4 Stitch on snap fasteners where indicated.

BIB AND BAGGY PANTS

Model 4

Fabric needed: 36″ (90cm) wide: ½yd (0.45m)
54″ (140cm) wide: ½yd (0.45m)
Notions: 3½yds (3.10m) bias binding, 2 buttons

Sewing instructions:

1 Reproduce the pattern on 2 x 2″ (5 x 5cm) dressmaker's pattern paper. If preferred, join the side seams together, then the bib can be cut out in one piece. Remember to plan for seam allowance.
2 With right sides together fold the fabric in half and pin the bib to it, having the middle of the front against the fabric fold.
3 Cut out the side and shoulder seams with an extra ⅜-¾″ (1-2cm) for seam allowance. Cut out the remaining edges without a seam allowance.

4 Zigzag around the edges of the pieces.
5 Stitch the shoulder seams and press them open.
6 Stitch bias binding around the armholes.
7 Stitch the side seams and press them open.
8 Stitch bias binding around the edge of the bib, at the same time stitching on a loop 2″ (5cm) from the neckline on the middle back edge. To make a loop, take 2½″ (6cm) of bias binding. Fold in half lengthwise and stitch around the edges. Form into a loop.
9 Finish off the neckline with bias binding. Allow 2½″ (6cm) extra binding to make a loop on one side of the opening, taking care to have both loops on the same side.
10 Sew buttons on, opposite the loops.

BAGGY PANTS

See description on page 41.

BIB WITH CAP SLEEVES

Model 5

Fabric needed: 36″ (90cm) wide: 1yd (0.90m); with this amount of fabric the middle front pattern is placed against the fabric fold
54″ (140cm) wide: 1yd (0.85m)
If pattern is laid out across width of the fabric: 36″ (90cm) wide: ½yd (0.40m)
54″ (140cm) wide: ½yd (0.40m)
Notions: 4yds (3.60m) bias binding

Sewing instructions:

1 Reproduce the bib on 2 x 2″ (5 x 5cm) dressmaker's pattern paper. Remember to plan for seam allowance.

64

2 Place the pattern twice on quilted fabric. You can use two different designs if preferred.
3 Cut along the middle front and middle back with an extra ⅜-¾" (1-2cm) for seam allowance. The neckline and the outer edge do not have a seam allowance.
4 Zigzag around the edge of the pieces.
5 Stitch the middle front seam together. Press the seam open.
6 Turn in the seam allowance of the middle back and stitch down ¼" (0.5cm) from the edge.
7 Stitch bias binding around the edge of the bib starting and finishing at the middle of the back. To make ties, cut four 12" (30cm) lengths of bias binding. Fold each one in half lengthwise and stitch around the edges. Stitch in place on both sides of the front and back panel.
8 Finish the neckline with bias binding. Allow 24" (60cm) more bias binding than needed for the neckline and leave 12" (30cm) loose on each side.

BIB WITH APPLIQUE   Model 6

Fabric needed: 36" (90cm) wide: 22" (55cm)
54" (140cm) wide: 22" (55cm)
If pattern is laid out across width of the fabric: 36" (90cm) wide: ½yd (0.40m)
54" (140cm) wide: ½yd (0.40m)
Notions: 2½yds (2.25m) bias binding, scraps of material for the applique

Sewing instructions:
1 Reproduce the pattern on 2 x 2" (5 x 5cm) dressmaker's pattern paper. Remember to plan for seam allowance.

2 With right sides together fold the fabric in half and pin the pattern to it, having the middle of the front against the fabric fold.
3 Cut out the bib without a seam allowance with the exception of the middle back which has a seam allowance of ⅜-¾" (1-2cm).
4 Zigzag around the edges of the bib.
5 Turn in the seam allowance on the middle back and stitch ¼" (0.5cm) from the edge.
6 Reproduce the drawing of the applique on 2 x 2" (5 x 5cm) dressmaker's pattern paper. Cut out the separate parts in fabric without seam allowances. Apply fusible webbing to the back of the parts. First place the flowered fabric on the bib and zigzag around the edges. Next come the bushes and last of all the sheep on top of the bushes and the flowers. Draw the head and the tail on the sheep and outline them in zigzag stitch or embroider them on.
7 Stitch bias binding around the edge of the bib, starting and finishing at the middle of the back.
8 Finish the neckline with bias binding. Allow 24" (60cm) more bias binding than you need for the neckline and leave 12" (30cm) loose on each side.

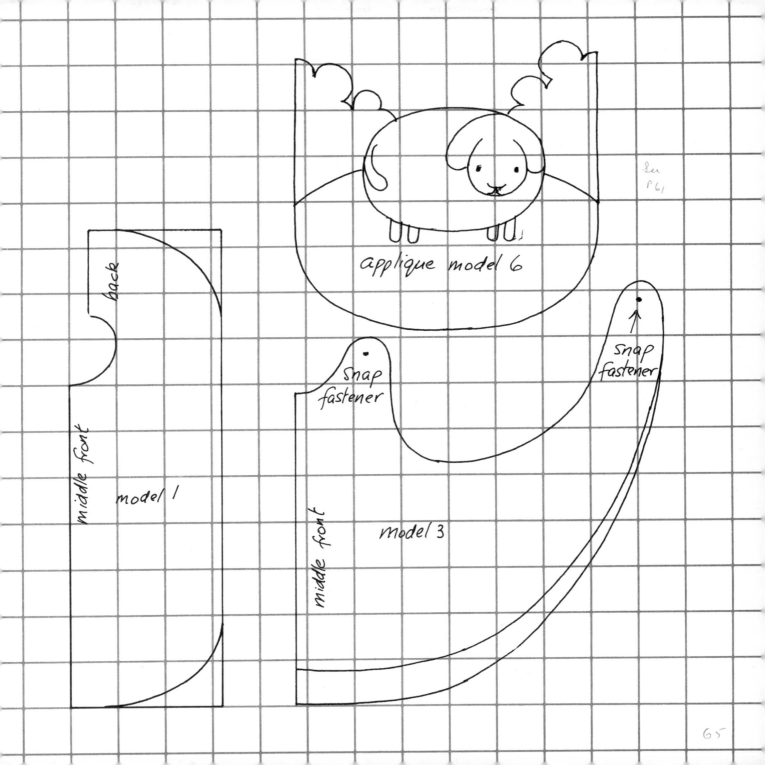

applique model 6

back

middle front

model 1

snap fastener

snap fastener

middle front

model 3

See P 61

65

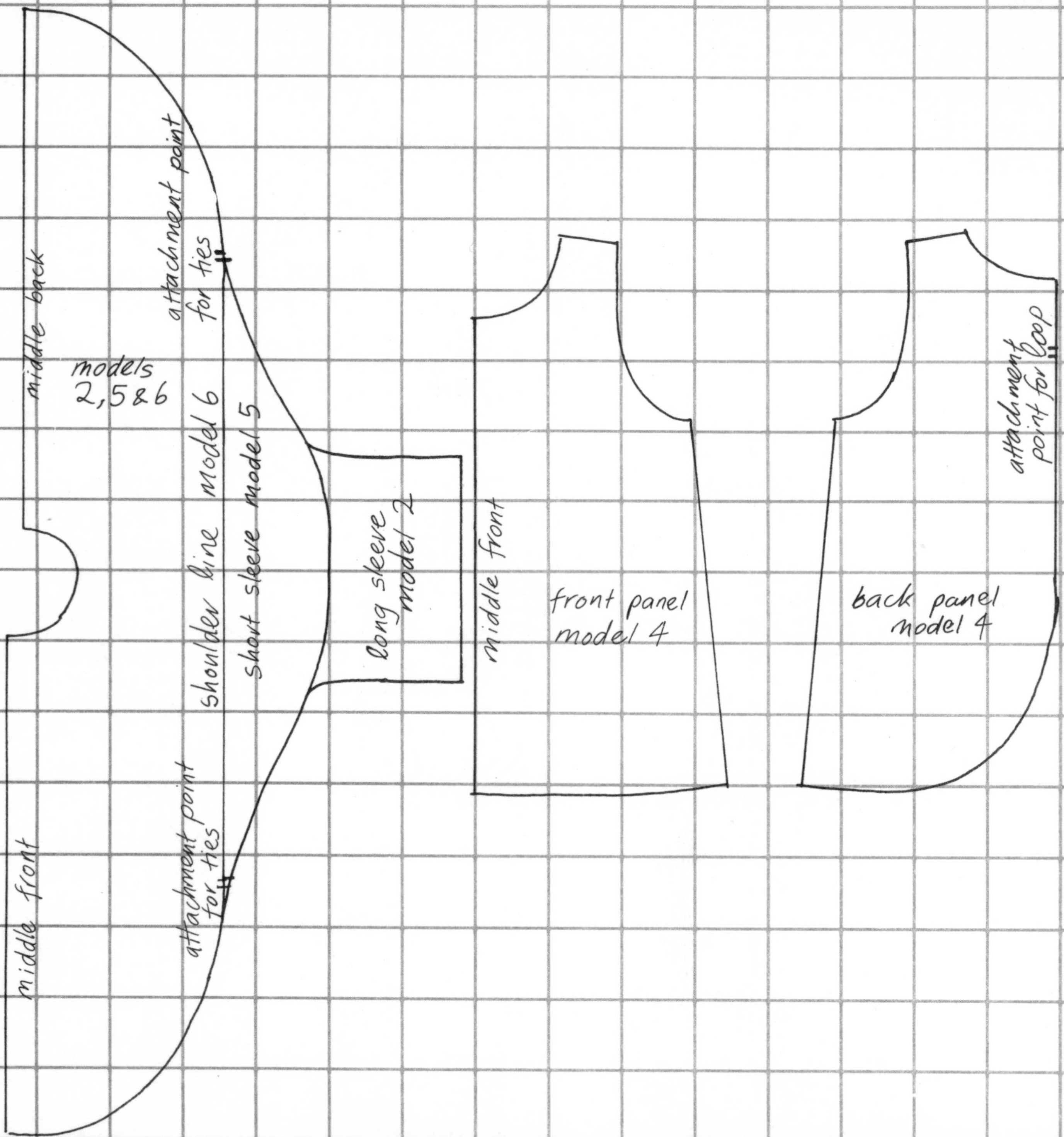

middle back

attachment point for ties

models
2, 5 & 6

shoulder line   model 6

short sleeve   model 5

long sleeve
model 2

middle front

attachment point
for ties

middle front

front panel
model 4

back panel
model 4

attachment point for loop

1   2   3   4

Coats and Jackets

Size by age:	0-3 months, 3-6 months, 6-9 months
Height of child:	24″ (62cm), 27″ (68cm), 29″ (74cm)
Fabrics:	Gabardine, twill, corduroy, needle-cord, velvet, glazed cotton.
	linings: flannel, acrylic fur.

JACKET WITH ZIPPER   Model 1

Pattern pieces:	front panel, back panel
Fabric needed:	36″ (90cm) wide:
	size 24″ (62cm): 1⅛yd (1.0m)
	sizes 27″ (68cm) & 29″ (74cm):
	2¼yds (2.0m)
	For the above amounts the middle is not placed on the fabric fold.
	54″ (140cm) wide, all sizes: 1⅛yd (1.0m)
Lining fabric:	you need the same amount of fabric for the lining
Notions:	an open-ended separating zipper measuring 10″ (26cm), 12″ (30cm) or 14″ (34cm), according to size of garment 2½yds (2.30m) bias binding,

Sewing instructions:

1 Reproduce the pattern pieces on 2 x 2″ (5 x 5cm) dressmaker's pattern paper. Remember to plan for seam allowance.

2 With right sides together fold the fabric in half and pin the pieces to it, having the middle of the back against the fabric fold if you are using 54″ (140cm) wide fabric.

3 For the cuffs, cut 2¾″ (7cm) extra on the end of the sleeves. Cut around the neckline without a seam allowance. Cut the bottom edge of the jacket with an extra 1⅜″ (3.5cm) for seam allowance. Cut along

the middle front with an extra ¾″ (2cm) for seam allowance. Allow an extra ⅜-¾″ (1-2cm) on the remaining edges for seam allowance.

4 Now fold the lining fabric in half and pin the pattern pieces to it. If you are using 54″ (140cm) wide fabric, remember to have the middle of the back against the fold. Cut out the pieces as described in step 3.

5 Zigzag around the edges of the pieces.

6 Stitch the underarm side seams and the upper arm seams together. Clip the curves in the seam allowance and press the seams open.

7 Stitch the underarm side seams and the upper arm seams of the lining fabric together. Clip the curves in the seam allowance and press the seams open.

8 With right sides together fit the two jackets into each other. Stitch the bottom edge of the sleeves together.

9 Turn the jacket right side out.

10 Turn in and iron the middle front seam allowance of the jacket. Do the same with the lining fabric. Baste the zipper between the two fabrics and then stitch it down, stopping 1″ (2.5cm) from the bottom edge. Leave the seam open on the bottom edge. (See p14 for how to insert zipper.)

11 Finish the neckline with bias binding. Allow 24″ (60cm) more than you need for the neckline and leave 12″ (30cm) loose on each side.

12 Turn in ⅜″ (1cm) around the bottom edge of both fabrics. Stitch together close to the edge.

13 Stitch again around the edge ⅝″ (1.5cm) from the first row.

14 Take 1½yds (1.30m) bias binding. Fold it in half lengthwise, stitch around the edges and thread it through the casing.

COAT AND BONNET   Model 2

Pattern pieces: front panel, back panel, collar
Fabric needed: 36″ (90cm) wide, sizes 24″ (62cm) and
27″ (68cm): 1⅛yd (1.10m)
36″ (90cm) wide, size 29″ (74cm):
2¼yds (2.10m)
In this case the middle back has a seam.
54″ (140cm) wide, all sizes: 1⅛yd (1.0m)
Lining fabric: you need the same amount of fabric
Notions: ½yd (40cm) elastic ⅜″ (1cm) wide,
snap fasteners

Sewing instructions:
1 Reproduce the pattern pieces on 2 x 2″ (5 x 5cm) dressmaker's pattern paper. Remember the overlap on the front panel and plan for seam allowance.
2 With right sides together fold the fabric in half and pin the pieces to it, having the middle of the back against the fabric fold (see the exception), and the neckline border also against the fabric fold.
3 Allow an extra 1⅜″ (3.5cm) along the bottom edge of the sleeves for seam allowance. Allow an extra ⅜-¾″ (1-2cm) along the remaining edges.
4 Fold the lining fabric in half and pin the pieces to it. See step 2. Cut out the pieces. See step 3.
5 Zigzag around the edges of the pieces.
6 Stitch the upper arm seams and the underarm side seams together. Clip the curve in the seam allowance and press the seams open.
7 Stitch the upper arm seams and the underarm side seams of the lining fabric. Clip the curve of the seam allowance. Press the seams open.
8 Stitch the collar to the coat. Clip the seam edge and iron the seam down.

9 Stitch the collar lining to the coat lining. Clip the seam allowance and iron the seam down.
10 With right sides together fit the two coats into each other.
11 Stitch the collars, the front panels and the bottom edges of the sleeves together. Leave an opening on the bottom edge of the sleeves to insert the elastic.
12 Clip the seam allowance of the collar.
13 Turn the coat right side out. Iron the collar, middle front and bottom edge of the sleeves flat.
14 Turn in ⅜″ (1cm) along the bottom edge of both fabrics.
15 Now top-stitch around the entire coat along the collar, middle front and hemline. In the process both fabrics are stitched together along the hemline.
16 Stitch around the bottom edge of the sleeves ⅝″ (1.5cm) from the edge.
17 Thread elastic through the opening in the bottom edge of the sleeves. Stitch the ends together and then stitch up the openings.
18 To fasten the jacket, stitch snap fasteners to the front panel.

BONNET

Follow instructions for "Bonnet with pompoms", Model 4 page 179, size 6 months – 2 years.

KIMONO-STYLE JACKET   Model 3

Pattern pieces: front panel, back panel
Fabric needed: 36″ (90cm) wide, size 24″ (62cm): 1¾yds (1.50m)
36″ (90cm) wide, sizes 27″ (68cm) and

29" (74cm): 1¼yds (2.0m)
In this case the middle back has a seam.
54" (140cm) wide, all sizes: 1¾yd (1.5m)

Lining fabric: you need the same amount of fabric
Notions: 5½yds (5m) bias binding

Sewing instructions:

1 Reproduce the pattern pieces on 2 x 2" (5 x 5cm) dressmaker's pattern paper. Remember the diagonal wrapover on the front panel and to plan for seam allowance.
2 With right sides together fold the fabric in half and pin the pieces to it, having the middle of the back against the fabric fold. See the exceptions. Cut out the sleeves with 2¾" (7cm) extra on the ends to make the cuffs. Cut out the neckline, the wrapover, the hemline and the bottom edge of the sleeves without seam allowances. Cut out the remaining edges with an extra ⅜-¾" (1-2cm).
3 Now fold the lining fabric in half and pin the pattern pieces to it, having the middle of the back against the fabric fold. See the exceptions. Cut out the pieces as described in step 2.
4 Zigzag around the edges of all the pieces.
5 Stitch the upper arm seams together. Press the seams open.
6 Stitch the upper arm seams of the lining fabric together. Press the seams open.
7 Decide which side should wrap over on top and then stitch the underarm side seams together. To make the tie, fold a 12" (30cm) length of bias binding in half lengthwise and stitch around the edges. Stitch this on where indicated, having the loose end for tying on the right side of the seam.

8 Stitch the underarm side seams of the lining fabric. See step 7.
9 With the wrong sides together fit both jackets into each other.
10 Stitch bias binding along the side of the wrapover and along the hemline. Make another two 12" (30cm) length ties from bias binding (see step 7) and stitch these 2" (5cm) from the top edge of the wrapover on both sides.
11 Stitch bias binding around the neckline and the upper edge of the wrapover. Allow 24" (60cm) more binding than the total length of the neckline and upper edge of wrapover and leave 12" (30cm) loose on both sides.
12 Finish off the bottom edges of the sleeves with bias binding.

COAT WITH HOOD   *Model 4*

Pattern pieces: front panel, back panel, hood
Fabric needed: 36" (90cm) wide: 1½yds (1.40m)
54" (140cm) wide: 1¼yds (1.10m)
Lining fabric: you need the same amount of fabric
Notions: snap fasteners

Sewing instructions:

Follow the sewing instructions for model 2, the only exception being step 3.
Substitute "hood" wherever "collar" is mentioned.
Steps 14 and 15 no longer apply.
 3 Cut out all pieces with an extra ⅜-¾" (1-2cm) for seam allowance.

COAT WITH ZIPPER AT THE BACK   *Model 5*

Pattern pieces: front panel, back panel, hood
Fabric needed: 36" (90cm) wide, size 24" (62cm):
1½yds (1.40m)
36" (90cm) wide, sizes 27" (68cm) and
29" (74cm): 2¼yds (2.00m)
54" (140cm) wide, all sizes: 1¼yds (1.10m)
Lining fabric: you need the same amount of fabric.
Notions: open-ended separating zipper measuring 30" (75cm), 32" (80cm), 34" (85cm)
according to size of garment

Sewing instructions:

1   Reproduce the pattern pieces on 2 x 2" (5 x 5cm)
dressmaker's pattern paper. Remember to plan for
seam allowance.
2   With right sides together fold the fabric in half and
pin the pieces to it, having the middle of the front
against the fabric fold. Cut out the sleeves with 2¾"
(7cm) extra on the ends for the cuffs. Cut out the
rest with an extra ⅜-¾" (1-2cm) for seam allowance.
3   Now fold the lining fabric in half and pin the pattern
pieces to it with the middle of the front against the
fabric fold. Cut out as described in step 2.
4   Zigzag around the edges of the pieces.
5   Stitch the underarm side seams and the upper arm
seams together. Clip the curves in the seam allowance and press the seams open.
6   Stitch the underarm side seams and the upper arm
seams of the lining fabric. Clip the curves in the
seam allowance and press the seams open.
7   Stitch the hood sections on to the neckline. Clip the
seam allowances and press the seams open.

8   Repeat step 7 with the lining fabric.
9   With right sides together, fit both jackets into each
other. Stitch the front of the hoods (lining and outer
layer) together and stitch the bottom edges of the
sleeves together.
10   Turn the coat right side out.
11   Turn in and iron the seam allowance of the top back
seam of the hood and the middle back seam. Do
the same with the lining fabric. Baste the zipper in
between both fabrics and stitch, finishing ¾" (2cm)
from the hemline. (see p14 for how to insert zipper.)
12   Turn in the hemline of both fabrics and stitch them
together along the edge. Join up this stitching with
the stitching of the zipper.

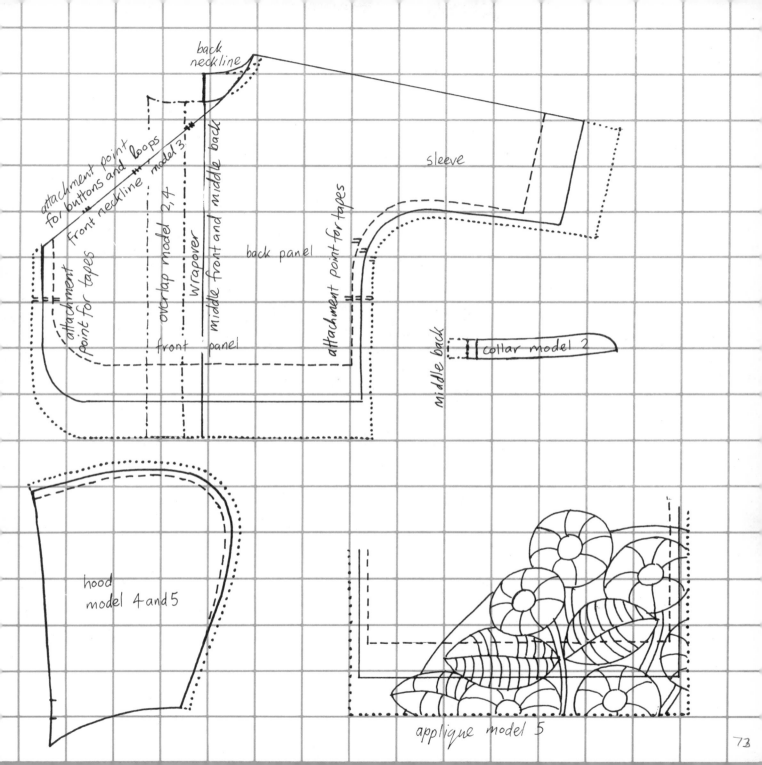

back
neckline

attachment point
for buttons and loops

front neckline model 3

attachment point for tapes

overlap model 2,4

front panel

wrapover

middle front and middle back

back panel

attachment point for tapes

sleeve

middle back

collar model 2

hood
model 4 and 5

applique model 5

73

1   2   3

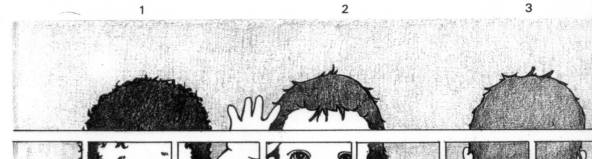

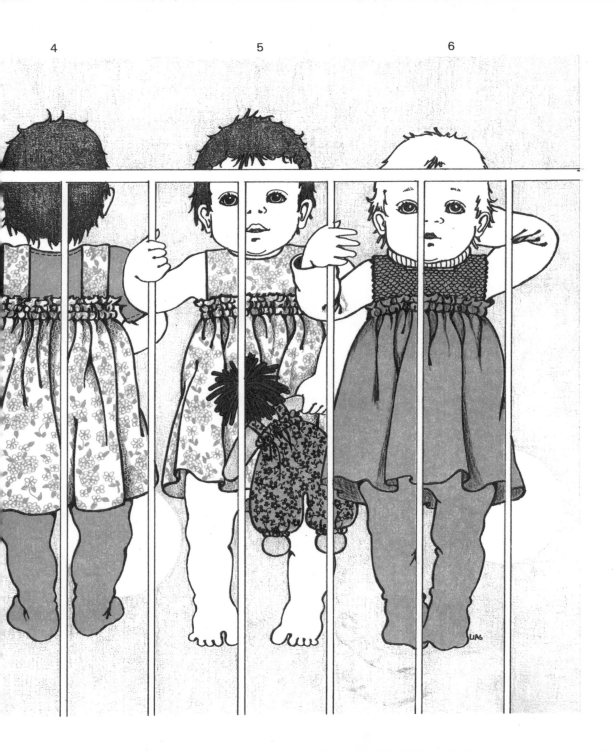

Dresses and pinafores

Size by age: *6-9 months, 18 months, 2 years*
Height of child: *29" (74cm), 34" (86cm), 36" (92cm)*
Fabrics: *Flowered cotton, plain cotton, batiste, flannel, viyella, seersucker, corduroy, velvet, embroidered cotton*

SKIRT

Pattern pieces: skirt front, skirt back
Fabric needed: 36" (0.90m) wide: ⅞yd (0.80m) or 1⅛yd (100cm) depending on length
                 54" (140cm) wide: ½yd (0.40m) or ⅝yd (0.50m) depending on length
Notions: 22" (55cm) elastic for casing

Sewing instructions: these apply to all models

1 Reproduce the skirt on 2 x 2" (5 x 5cm) dressmaker's pattern paper. Reproduce only half of the pattern if you are using a 36" (90cm) wide fabric. Remember to plan for seam allowance.
2 With right sides together, fold the fabric in half and pin the pattern to it. If using a 36" (90cm) wide fabric, the middle of the front and middle of the back are placed against the fabric fold. If using 54" (140cm) wide fabric, place a side seam against the fabric fold.
3 Cut around the pattern with an extra ⅜-¾" (1-2cm) for seam allowance. The upper part of the pattern has an allowance for three casings. If more casings are preferred then add more seam allowance.
4 Zigzag around the edges of the pieces.
5 Stitch the side seams together. At the top of the skirt leave 2" (5cm) open on one of the seams. Press the seams open.
6 Fold over 2¼" (6cm) on the top edge of the skirt and iron it flat.
7 Stitch ⅜" (1cm) from the top edge.
8 Stitch again, ⅜" (1cm) underneath the first row. For each additional casing you stitch another row ⅜" (1cm) underneath the previous row.
9 Thread the elastic into the casing or casings. Stitch the two ends of the elastic together and then stitch up the opening(s).
10 Fold in the hemline and stitch ¼" (0.5cm) from the bottom edge of the skirt.

SKIRT WITH SHOULDER TIES   Model 1

Notions: 1¾yd (1.60m) bias binding

Sewing instructions:
1 Sew the skirt according to the instructions.
2 To make ties, fold bias binding in half lengthwise and stitch around the edges. Cut into four equal lengths and stitch to the front and the back of the skirt. The ties on the front are 5½" (14cm) apart. The ties on the back are 1½" (4cm) apart.

SUNDRESS OR PINAFORE WITH APPLIQUE
Model 2 and 3

Pattern pieces: front top panel, back top panel
Fabric needed: no extra fabric needed if the fabric is 36" (90cm) wide
                 ¼yd (16cm) extra fabric if the fabric is 54" (140cm) wide
Notions: 3yds (2.80m) bias binding

Sewing instructions:

1 Sew the skirt according to the instructions.
2 Reproduce the front and back top panels on 2 x 2″ (5 x 5cm) dressmaker's pattern paper. Remember to plan for seam allowance.
3 With right sides together, fold the fabric in half and pin the pieces to it, having the middle of the front and middle of the back against the fabric fold.
4 Cut out the top and bottom edges with an extra ¾″ (2cm) for seam allowance. Cut out the sides without a seam allowance. Zigzag around the edges of the pieces.
5 Reproduce the applique drawing on 2 x 2″ (5 x 5cm) dressmaker's pattern paper. Cut out the different sections in contrasting fabrics without a seam allowance. Don't use very thick fabric. Apply fusible webbing to the back of the pieces. Pin the applique pieces on to the front and back panels and zigzag around the edges. Stitch along the top edge of the panels.
6 Stitch bias binding along the side edges. On each side allow 12″ (30cm) more bias binding than the length of the side. Leave 12″ (30cm) loose at the top for tying in a bow.
7 Place the middle of the top front panel against the middle of the skirt front.
8 Stitch it on ⅜″ (1cm) from the top edge of the skirt.
9 Place the middle of the top back panel against the middle of the back of the skirt.
10 Stitch it on ⅜″ (1cm) from the top edge of the skirt.

SLEEVELESS DRESS OR PINAFORE *Model 4 and 5*

Pattern piece: bib

Fabric needed: 36″ (90cm) wide: ⅜yd (0.32m) plus the fabric for the skirt
54″ (140cm) wide: ⅜yd (0.32m) plus the fabric for the skirt

Sewing instructions:

1 Sew the skirt according to the instructions.
2 Reproduce the pattern for the bib on 2 x 2″ (5 x 5cm) dressmaker's pattern paper. Remember to plan for seam allowance.
3 With right sides together fold the material for the bib in half and pin the pattern to it, having the middle of the front against the fabric fold.
4 Cut out the pattern twice, with an extra ¾″ (2cm) for seam allowance on the bottom edges. Allow an extra ⅜-¾″ (1-2cm) on the remaining edges for seam allowance.
5 Zigzag around the edges of the pieces.
6 With right sides together, stitch along the sides and top edge. The bottom edge is not stitched.
7 Clip the seam allowance in the curve of the neckline, turn right side out and iron flat.
8 Place the middle front of the bib against the middle front of the skirt.
9 Stitch on ⅜″ (1cm) from the top edge of the skirt.
10 Place each shoulder strap 1½″ (4cm) from the middle back seam of the skirt, so that there is a total distance of 3″ (8cm) between the two straps.
11 Stitch them on ⅜″ (1cm) from the top edge.

DRESS OR PINAFORE WITH KNITTED BODICE
Model 6

Notions: knitting yarn, knitting needles

Sewing instructions:

1 Sew the skirt according to the instructions.
2 Reproduce the bodice front panel and bodice back panel on on 2 x 2" (5 x 5cm) dressmaker's pattern paper. Lay the pieces on a piece of folded paper and cut around them.
3 In a plain stitch, knit a bodice front panel and bodice back panel to match the pattern pieces, making them ¾" (2cm) longer than the pattern pieces.
4 Place the middle of the bodice front against the middle of the skirt front.
5 Stitch on ⅜" (1cm) from the top edge of the skirt.
6 Place the middle of the bodice back against the middle of the skirt back.
7 Stitch on ⅜" (1cm) from the top edge of the skirt.
8 Turn the dress inside out and sew the shoulder seams together.

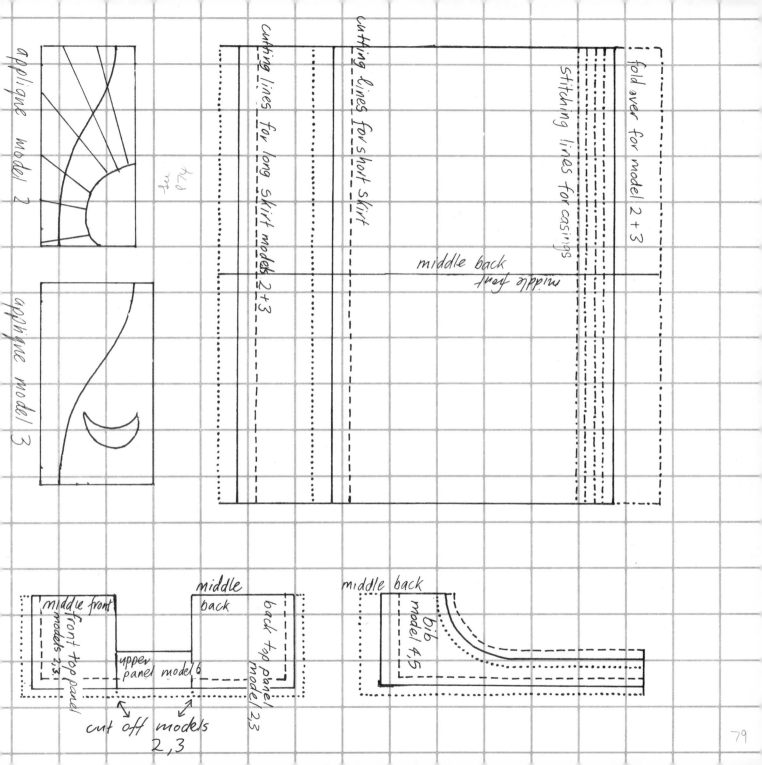

applique model 2

applique model 3

cutting lines for long skirt models 2+3

cutting lines for short skirt

stitching lines for casings

fold over for model 2 + 3

middle back

middle front

middle front

middle back

front top panel models 2,3

upper panel model 6

back top panel model 2,3

cut off models 2,3

middle back

bib model 4,5

79

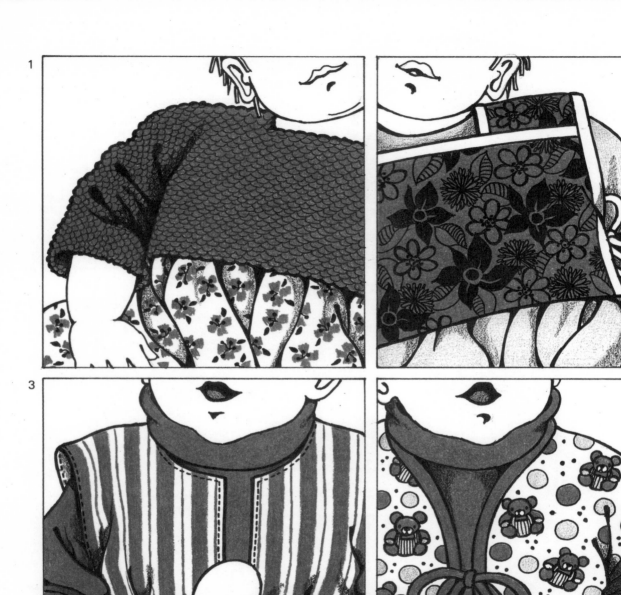

5

6

81

All kinds of tops

Size by age: *6-9 months, 18 months, 3 years*
Height of child: *29" (74cm),   34" (86cm), 38" (98cm)*
Fabrics: *Printed cotton, flannel, jacquard, corduroy, velvet, velveteen, quilted cotton Glazed cotton lined with flannel, jacquard lined with flannel.*

KNITTED TOP   Model 1

Pattern pieces: front panel, back panel
Notions: knitting yarn and knitting needles

Instructions:
1 Reproduce the pattern pieces on 2 x 2" (5 x 5cm) dressmaker's pattern paper.
2 Fold a piece of paper in half and pin the pieces to it, having the middle of the front and middle of the back against the fold. Cut out the pieces without a seam allowance.
3 Knit in a plain stitch to match the pattern pieces.
4 Sew the seams together.

You can also use this pattern on an old pullover.

TOP WITH SIDE FASTENINGS   Model 2

Pattern pieces: front panel, back panel, shoulder sections
Fabric needed: 36" (90cm) wide: ⅜yd (0.30m)
                   54" (140cm) wide: ⅜yd (0.30m)
Notions: 3½yd (3.20m) bias binding

Sewing instructions:
1 Reproduce the pattern pieces on 2 x 2" (5 x 5cm) dressmaker's pattern paper. Remember to plan for

seam allowance. Join the tops of the front and back shoulder sections together and cut out as one piece.
2 With right sides together fold the fabric in half and pin the pieces to it, having the middle of the front and middle of the back against the fabric fold.
3 Cut out the pieces. Cut out the sides of the front and back panels and the sides of the shoulder sections without a seam allowance. Cut out the top edge of the front and back panels and the lower edge of the shoulder sections with an extra ¼" (0.5cm) for seam allowance. The hemline with an extra ⅜-¾" (1-2cm) for seam allowance.
4 Zigzag around the edges of the pieces.
5 Finish the inside of the shoulder sections and the top edge of the front and back panels with bias binding.
6 Stitch the shoulder sections to the front and back panels, taking care that the bias binding on the front and back panels is on the right side of the garment.
7 Finish the sides with bias binding. To make the ties, cut four 12" (30cm) lengths of bias binding. Fold each one in half lengthwise and stitch around the edges. Stitch the ties to the front and back as indicated on the pattern.
8 Turn in ¾" (2cm) along the hemlines and stitch.

SLEEVELESS TOP WITH TIE WAIST   Model 3

Pattern pieces: front panel, back panel
Fabric needed: 36" (90cm) wide: ¾yd (0.70m)
                   54" (140cm) wide: ⅜yd (0.35m)
Lining fabric: 36" (90cm) wide: ¾yd (0.70m)
                   54" (140cm) wide: ⅜yd (0.35m)
Notions: 1½yd (1.40m) cord

Sewing instructions:
1 Reproduce the pattern pieces on 2 x 2″ (5 x 5cm) dressmaker's pattern paper. Remember to plan for seam allowance. Mark the position of the casing.
2 With right sides together fold the fabric in half and pin the pattern pieces to it, having the middle of the back against the fabric fold. Cut out the pieces with an extra ⅜-¾″ (1-2cm) for seam allowance.
3 Repeat step 2 with lining fabric.
4 Zigzag around the edges of the pieces.
5 Stitch the seams together. Clip the curves in the seam allowance and press the seams open.
6 Repeat step 5 with lining fabric.
7 With right sides together, fit the lining into the outer fabric. Mark the position where the casing is to be stitched on the front panel.
8 Now stitch the inside and outside together. Also stitch the armholes together. Leave open where the casing is to be on the front. Leave the hemline open. Cut off the corners of the seam edges diagonally and clip the seam allowance of the neckline. Turn the garment right side out and iron it flat.
9 Do two rows of stitching around the waistline as indicated on the pattern. This will form the casing.
10 Turn in the hemline of the outer fabric and the hemline of the lining fabric and stitch these together ¼″ (0.5cm) from the bottom edge.
11 Top-stitch around the armholes, neckline and the front edges. Leave the casing open.
12 Thread the cord through the casing.

SHORT SLEEVED BOLERO-TYPE JACKET Model 4

Pattern pieces: front panel, back panel

Fabric needed: 36″ (90cm) wide: ¾yd (0.60m)
                         54″ (140cm) wide: ⅜yd (0.30m)
Notions: 2⅞yd (2.60m) bias binding

Sewing instructions:
1 Reproduce the pattern pieces on 2 x 2″ (5 x 5cm) dressmaker's pattern paper. Remember to plan for seam allowance.
2 With right sides together fold the fabric in half and pin the pattern pieces to it, having the middle of the back against the fabric fold.
3 Cut out the shoulder seams and the side seams with an extra ⅜-¾″ (1-2cm) for seam allowance, the remaining edges without a seam allowance.
4 Zigzag around the edges of the pieces.
5 Stitch the seams together. Clip the curve in the seam allowance and press the seams open.
6 Stitch bias binding around the armholes.
7 To make ties, cut two 12″ (30cm) lengths of bias binding. Fold in half lengthwise and stitch around the edges. Attach to the front panels as indicated on the pattern.
8 Stitch bias binding around the edges of the garment, stitching on ties at the same time.

SHORT SLEEVELESS BOLERO Model 5

Pattern pieces: front panel, back panel
Fabric needed: 36″ (90cm) wide: ¾yd (0.60m)
                         54″ (140cm) wide: ⅜yd (0.30m)
Notions: 2⅞yd (2.60m) bias binding

Sewing instructions:
Follow the instructions for model 4. The only difference is in step 8 and step 9 is added.

8 Stitch bias binding around the edges of the garment starting at the middle front neckline on one side and finishing at the middle front neckline on the other side.

9 Stitch bias binding around the neckline. Allow 24" (60cm) more bias binding than you need for the neckline and leave 12" (30cm) loose on each side.

SLEEVELESS BOLERO WITHOUT TIES   *Model 6*

Pattern pieces: front panel, back panel
Fabric needed: 36" (90cm) wide: ¾yd (0.70m)
54" (140cm) wide: ⅜yd (0.35m)
Notions: 2½yds (2.25m) bias binding

Sewing instructions:
Follow the instructions for model 4. Omit step 7 and the reference to ties in step 8.

front panel
models 3,6

casing model 3

middle front

middle back

back panel
model 3,6

casing model 3

mark position of
casing on pattern

front panel
model 4, 5

middle front

attachment point for tape model 4

middle back

back panel
model 4, 5

See P 91

3

Playsuits

Size by age:	*6-9 months, 18 months, 3 years*
Height of child:	*29" (74cm), 34" (86cm), 38" (98cm)*
Fabrics:	*Soft fabrics, printed or plain, flannel, seersucker, corduroy, velveteen.*

PLAYSUIT   *Model 1*

Pattern pieces: pants front, pants back, bib
Fabric needed: 36" (90cm) wide: 1⅞yd (1.75m)
54" (140cm) wide: 1⅛yd (0.95m)
Notions: 4yds (3.70m) bias binding,
20" (50cm) elastic ⅜" (1cm) wide

Sewing instructions:

1 Reproduce the pattern pieces on 2 x 2" (5 x 5cm) dressmaker's pattern paper. Remember to plan for seam allowance.
2 With right sides together fold the fabric in half and pin the pieces to it, having the middle front of the bib against the fabric fold.
3 The upper edge of the pants back and the armholes of the bib are cut out without a seam allowance. Allow an extra 2" (5cm) along the bottom edge of the legs for seam allowance. Allow an extra ⅜-¾" (1-2cm) for seam allowance on the remaining edges.
4 Zigzag around the edges of the pieces.
5 Stitch the inside leg seams of the pants front and pants back together. Press the seams open.
6 Stitch the crotch seams together. Clip the curve in the seam allowance. Press the seam open.
7 Stitch the side seams together, leaving 2¼" (6cm) open at the top. Press the seams open.
8 Turn in 1" (2.5cm) along the bottom edges of the legs and stitch ⅝" (1.5cm) from the bottom edge. Leave a small opening. Thread the elastic through. Stitch the two ends of the elastic together and then stitch up the opening.
9 Gather the upper edge of the pants until both the front and the back panel are the same width as the bib.
10 With right sides together, stitch the bib to the pants front. Turn in and stitch the seam allowance of the side openings and the side edges of the bib.
11 Turn in and stitch the top edge of the bib.
12 Stitch bias binding along the waistline at the back of the pants. Allow 24" (60cm) more bias binding than you need for the width and leave 12" (30cm) loose on both sides. At the same time, stitch on the back straps made from two 20" (50cm) lengths of bias binding. To make the straps fold the lengths of binding in half lengthwise and stitch around the edges. Stitch them on to the middle of the back 1½" (4cm) apart from each other.
13 Stitch bias binding around the armholes of the bib. Allow 28" (70cm) more than you need for the arm-hole and leave 12" (30cm) loose on the sides and 16" (40cm) loose at the top.

PLAYSUIT WITH OR WITHOUT APPLIQUE
Model 2 and 3

Pattern pieces: pants front, pants back, bib
Fabric needed: 36" (90cm) wide: 1⅞yd (1.75m)
54" (140cm) wide: 1⅛yd (0.95m)
Notions: 4yds (3.70m) bias binding,
20" (50cm) elastic ⅜" (1cm) wide

Sewing instructions:

Follow the instructions for model 1. The only variations are in steps 2, 3 and 12.

2 With right sides together fold the fabric in half, pin the pattern pieces to it. The bib is cut out twice. Place the bib against the fabric fold each time.

3 Allow an extra 2" (5cm) for seam allowance at the bottom edge of the legs. Cut out the armholes of both bibs without a seam allowance. Allow an extra ⅜-¾" (1-2cm) for seam allowance on the remaining edges. If desired, prepare the applique illustrated in model 2.(See instructions below.)

12 With right sides together stitch the bib to the pants back. Turn in and stitch the top edge of the bib. Turn in and stitch the seam allowance of the side openings and the side edges of the bib.

Instructions for the applique on the bib for model 2:
Reproduce the drawing of the applique on 2 x 2" (5 x 5cm) dressmaker's pattern paper. Cut the separate pieces out in fabric. Don't use very thick fabric. Apply fusible webbing to the backs of the pieces. Place the applique on to the bib and zigzag in place around the edges.

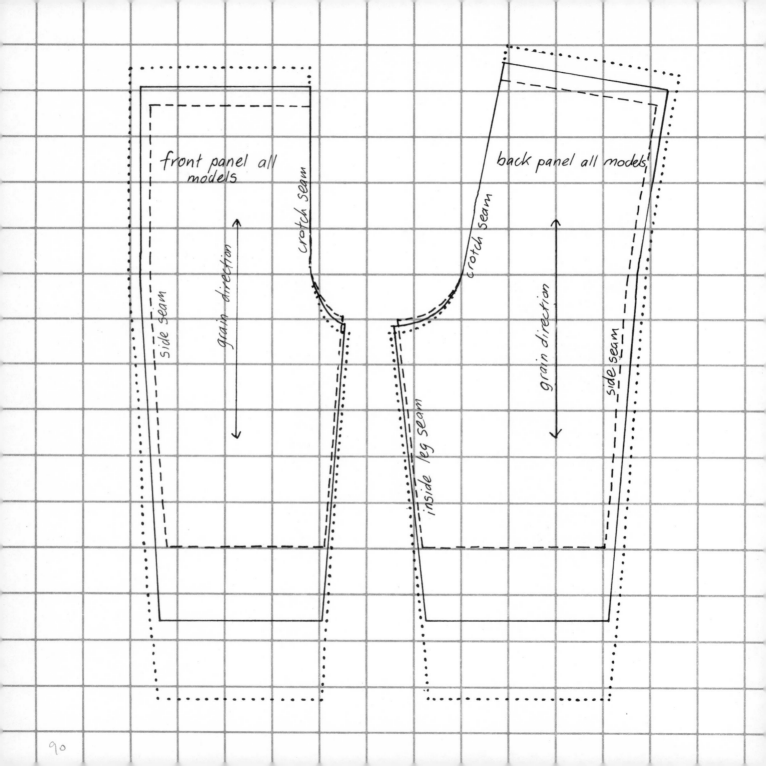

front panel all
models

side seam

grain direction

crotch seam

crotch seam

inside leg seam

grain direction

side seam

back panel all models

90

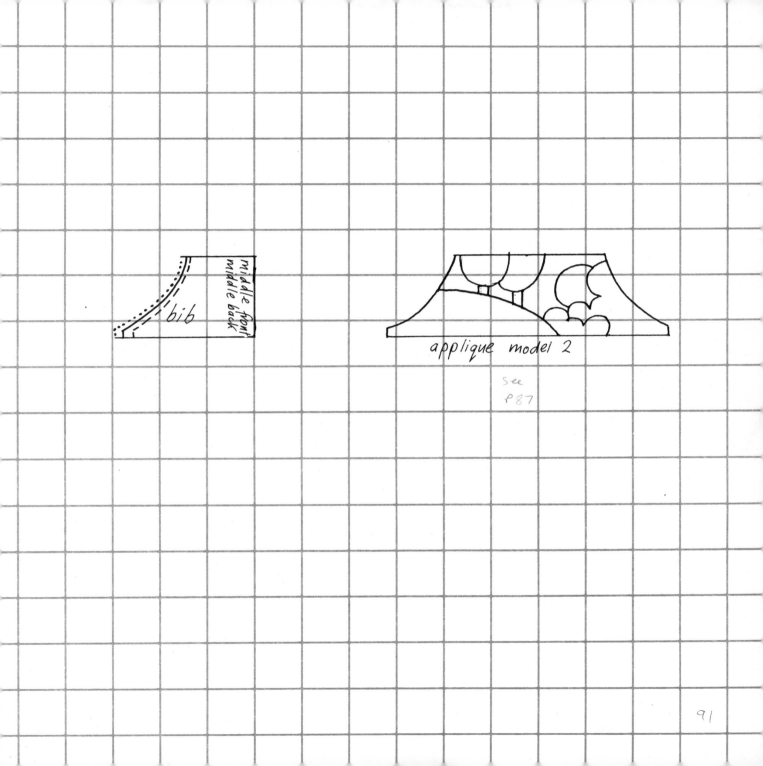

bib

middle front
middle back

applique model 2

see
p87

91

4

5

6

Sep 99

LIAS

93

Tops and T-shirts

Size by age: *9-12 mths,   2 years,   4 years*
Height of child: *32" (80cm), 36" (92cm), 40" (104cm)*
Fabrics: *Stretch fabrics such as: jersey, terry-cloth, tricot or soft fabrics such as flannel.*

Stretch fabrics should always be stitched with a gentle zigzag stitch. This gives the seam some elasticity.

KIMONO-STYLE TOP WITH KNITTED CUFFS
Model 1

Pattern pieces: front panel with wrapover, back panel
Fabric needed: 54" (140cm) wide: 1⅛yd (1.0m)
Notions: knitted cuffs for the sleeves and the bottom edge. These can be bought ready-made, or you can knit them yourself from remnants of wool yarn. 1½yd (1.35m) bias binding, 5 buttons

Sewing instructions:
1 Reproduce the pattern on 2 x 2" (5 x 5cm) dressmaker's pattern paper. Remember to plan for seam allowance.
2 With right sides together fold the fabric in half and pin the pieces to it, having the middle of the back against the fabric fold.
3 Cut out the neckline and the upper edge of the wrapover without a seam allowance. Cut out the remaining edges with an extra ⅜-¾" (1-2cm).
4 Zigzag around the edges of the pieces.
5 Stitch the upper arm seams together. Press the seams open.
6 Decide which side you want to wrap over. Finish the neckline and the upper edges of the wrapover with bias binding. At the same time, stitch on 5 loops where indicated. To make the loops, measure the amount of bias binding needed for each button. Cut a length for 5 loops. Fold the binding in half and stitch around the edges. Cut into 5 equal pieces.
7 Stitch the underarm side seams together, at the same time stitching the edge of the wrapover on both sides in with the side seam. Clip the curves in the seam allowance. Press the seams open.
8 Stitch the knitted cuffs on to the sleeves.
9 Stitch the knitted cuff around the bottom edge.
10 Sew the buttons on opposite the loops.

LONG-SLEEVED TOP WITH SHOULDER TIES
Model 2

Pattern pieces: front panel, back panel
Fabric needed: 54" (140cm) wide: 1⅛yd (1.0m)
Notions: 1¾yd (1.60m) bias binding, 1⅝yd (1.50m) elastic ⅜" (1cm) wide

Sewing instructions:
1 Reproduce the pattern pieces on 2 x 2" (5 x 5cm) dressmaker's pattern paper. Remember to plan for seam allowance.
2 With right sides together fold the fabric in half and pin the pieces to it, having both pieces on the fold.
3 Cut out the neckline without a seam allowance. Cut out the lower edge of the top and the lower edges of the sleeves with an extra 1" (2.5cm) for seam allowance. Cut out the remaining edges with an extra ⅜-¾" (1-2cm) for seam allowance.
4 Zigzag around the edges of the pieces.

5 Stitch the underarm side seams together. Clip the curve in the seam allowance and press the seams open.

6 Stitch the upper arm seams together, leaving a 2¼" (6cm) opening at the neckline of both seams. Press the seams open. Turn in and stitch the edges of the openings.

7 Finish the neckline with bias binding. Allow 24" (60cm) more bias binding than you need for the front and back necklines. Leave 12" (30cm) loose on both sides.

8 Fold in 1" (2.5cm) along the bottom edges of the sleeves and stitch round ⅝" (1.5cm) from the bottom edge. Leave a small opening. Thread the elastic into the opening. Stitch the two ends of elastic together and then stitch up the opening.

PLAIN TOP WITH BUTTON FASTENING   *Model 3*

Pattern pieces: front panel, back panel
Fabric needed: 54" (140cm) wide: 1⅛yd (1.0m)
Notions: 32" (80cm) bias binding, 6 buttons

Sewing instructions:

1 Reproduce the pattern pieces on 2 x 2" (5 x 5cm) dressmaker's pattern paper. Remember to plan for seam allowance.

2 With right sides together fold the fabric in half and pin the pieces to it, having both pieces on the fold.

3 Cut out the neckline without a seam allowance. Cut out the remaining edges with an extra ⅜-¾" (1-2cm) for seam allowance.

4 Zigzag around the edges of the pieces.

5 Stitch the underarm side seams together. Clip the curve in the seam allowance and press the seams open.

6 Stitch the upper arm seams together, leaving a 2¼" (6cm) opening in both seams at the neckline. Press the seams open. Turn in and stitch the edges of the openings. At the same time, stitch two loops of bias binding at the front of each opening. To make the loops, measure the amount of bias binding needed for each button. Cut a length to make four loops. Fold the binding in half and stitch around the edges. Cut into four.

7 Finish the neckline of the front and back panels with bias binding. Allow 5" (12cm) more bias binding than you need for the front and back necklines. Leave 2½" (6cm) loose on each side and make a loop out of this. Sew the buttons to the other edge of the opening, opposite the loops.

8 Turn in and stitch the bottom edge of the sleeves.

9 Turn in and stitch the bottom edge of the garment.

T-SHIRT WITH SHORT SLEEVES   *Model 4*

Pattern pieces: front panel, back panel
Fabric needed: 54" (140cm) wide: ½yd (0.50m)
Notions: 1⅛yd (1.0m) bias binding

Sewing instructions:
Follow the instructions for model 3. The only variations are in steps 6 and 7.

6 Stitch the upper arm seams together. Leave an opening 2¼" (6cm) at the neckline of one seam. Press the seams open. Turn in and stitch the edges of the opening.

7 Finish the neckline with bias binding. Allow 24" (60cm) more bias binding than you need for the neckline and leave 12" (30cm) loose on both sides of the opening.

T-SHIRT WITH APPLIQUE *Model 5*

Pattern pieces: front panel, back panel
Fabric needed: 54″ (140cm) wide: 1⅛yd (1.0m)
Notions: ¾yd (65cm) bias binding, 1⅝yd (1.50m) elastic ⅜″ (1cm) wide, 4 buttons

Sewing instructions:

Follow the instructions for model 2. Step 4a is added and there are variations in steps 6 and 7.

4a Reproduce the drawing of the applique on 2 x 2″ (5 x 5cm) dressmaker's pattern paper. Cut out the various sections in fabric without a seam allowance. Don't use very thick fabric. Apply fusible webbing to the backs of the pieces. Pin the applique in place on the front panel and zigzag around the edges. Zigzag the sun's rays on to the front panel (if preferred draw them on the front panel first with tailor's chalk).

6 Stitch the upper arm seams together. Leave an opening 2¼″ (6cm) at the neckline of both seams. Press the seams open. Turn in and stitch around the openings. At the same time stitch a loop of bias binding on the front edge on both sides. To make the loops, measure the amount of bias binding needed for each button and then cut a length to make two loops. Fold the binding in half lengthwise and stitch around the edges. Cut the tape in half and form into loops.

7 Finish the neckline with bias binding. Allow 4½″ (12cm) more bias binding than you need for the front neckline and leave 2¼″ (6cm) of tape loose on both sides of the neckline for loops. Sew on the buttons opposite the loops.

KIMONO-STYLE TOP WITH ELASTICATED SLEEVES *Model 6*

Pattern pieces: front panel, back panel
Fabric needed: 54″ (140cm) wide: 1⅛yd (1.0m)
Notions: 1½yd (1.35m) bias binding, 6 buttons, 20″ (50cm) elastic ⅜″ (1cm) wide, 22″ (55cm) ruched lingerie elastic ¾″ (2cm) wide

Sewing instructions:

Follow the instructions for model 1. The only variations are in steps 3, 8, 9 and 10.

3 Cut out the neckline and the top edge of the wrapover without a seam allowance. Cut out the bottom edge of the sleeves with an extra 1″ (2.5cm) for seam allowance. The remaining edges with an extra ⅜-¾″ (1-2cm) for seam allowance.

8 Turn in 1″ (2.5cm) along the bottom edge of the sleeves and stitch ⅝″ (1.5cm) from the bottom edge. Leave a small opening. Insert the elastic and stitch both ends together. Stitch up the opening.

9 Turn in ⅜″ (1cm) along the hemline and stitch around ¼″ (0.5cm) from the edge.

10 Stitch the ruched lingerie elastic all the way around the waistline.

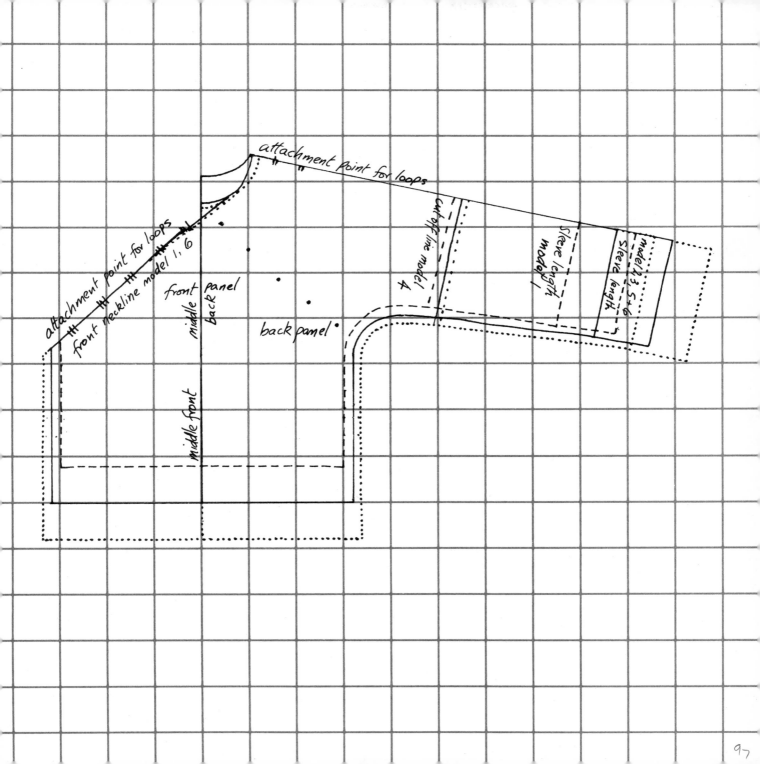

attachment point for loops

front neckline model 1, 6

attachment point for loops

front panel

middle back

middle front

back panel

cut off line model 4

sleeve length model 1

sleeve length model 2, 3, 5 + 6

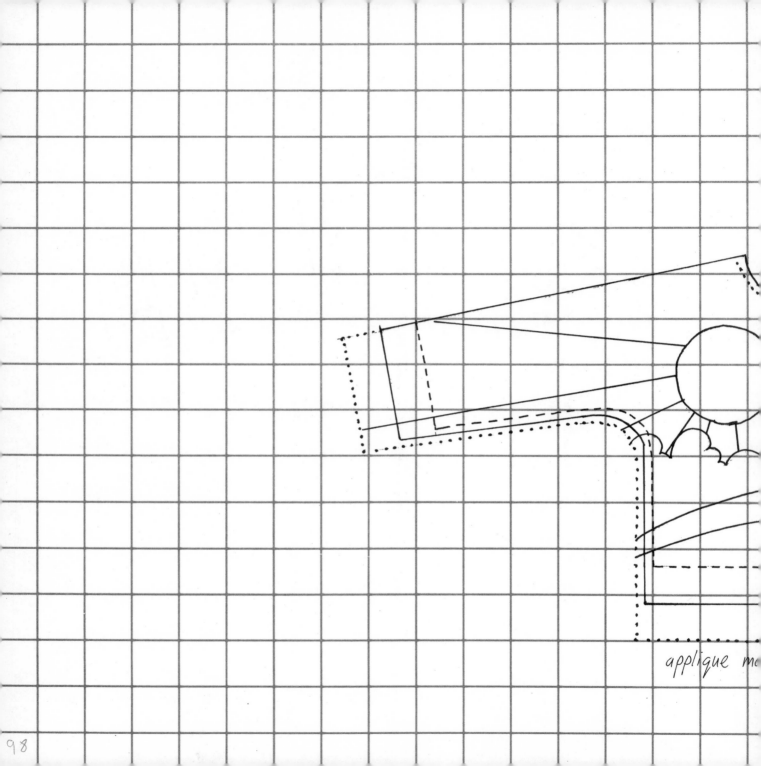

applique me

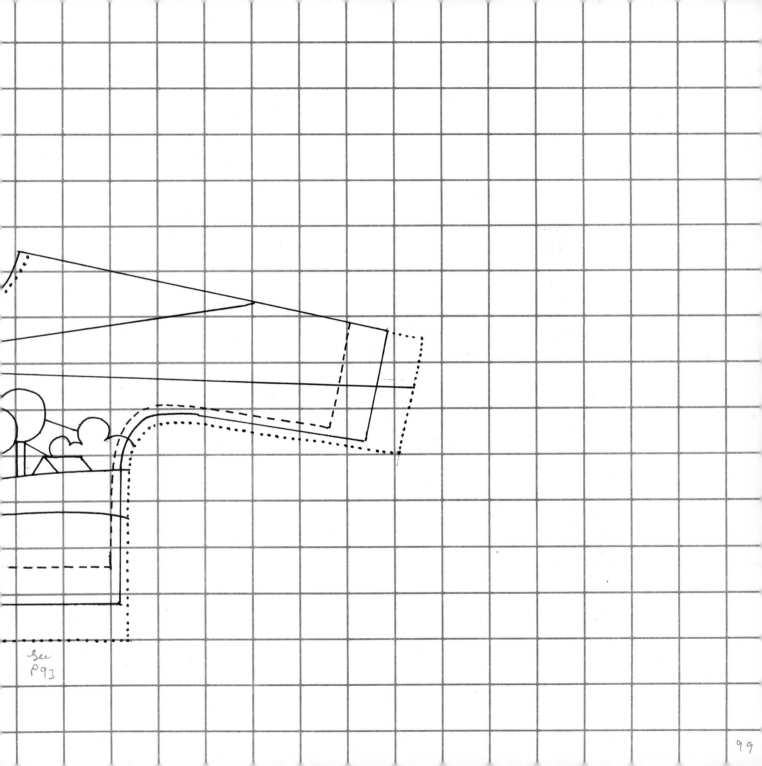

See
P93

Overalls

Size by age: *9-12 mths, 2 years,   4 years*
Height of child: *31″ (80cm), 36″ (92cm), 40″ (104cm)*
Fabrics: *Sturdy material such as: corduroy, ticking, denim, needlecord, velveteen.*

OVERALLS WITH SHOULDER TIES   *Model 1*

Pattern pieces: pants front, pants back
Fabric needed: 36″ (90cm) wide: 2⅛yd (1.90m)
               54″ (140cm) wide: 1¼yd (1.10m)
Notions: 5¾yd (5.25m) bias binding, 24″ (60cm) ruched lingerie elastic ¾″ (2cm) wide

Sewing instructions:
1 Reproduce the pattern pieces on 2 x 2″ (5 x 5cm) dressmaker's pattern paper. Mark the waistline and remember to plan for seam allowance.
2 With right sides together, fold the fabric in half and pin the pieces to it.
3 Cut out the bib and the armholes without a seam allowance, middle front and middle back with an extra ¼″ (0.5cm) for seam allowance. Cut out 2″ (5cm) extra on the bottom edge. Cut out the remaining edges with an extra ⅜-¾″ (1-2cm).
4 Zigzag around the edges of the pieces.
5 Stitch the inside leg seams of the pants front and pants back together. Press the seams open.
6 With the wrong sides together stitch the middle front and middle back together all the way around. The seam must be on the right side of the fabric. Clip the curve in the seam.
7 Cover the middle front and middle back seam on the right side with bias binding.
8 Stitch the side seams of the pants together. Leave 2¼″ (6cm) of the seam open next to the armholes to make the openings.

9 Turn in and stitch around the openings.
10 Stitch bias binding along both bib tops.
11 Stitch bias binding around the armholes. Allow 28″ (70cm) more bias binding than you need for each armhole and leave 16″ (40cm) loose at the top and 12″ (30cm) at the bottom.
12 Gather the lower edge of each leg until it has a circumference of 8″ (20cm).
13 Stitch bias binding around the edge of each leg.
14 Stitch ¾″ (2cm) wide ruched lingerie elastic around the waistline where indicated on the pattern.

OVERALLS WITH METAL CLASPS   *Model 4*

Pattern pieces: pants front, pants back, shoulder band, front facing, back facing
Fabric needed: 36″ (90cm) wide: 2⅝yd (2.40m)
               54″ (140cm) wide: 1½yd (1.35m)
Notions: 12″ (30cm) ruched lingerie elastic ¾″ (2cm) wide, 2 metal clasps

Sewing instructions:
Follow the instructions for models 2 and 3, the only variation being in step 15. The pocket can be left out.
15 Sew buttons on to the bib and attach metal clasps to the two shoulder bands.

OVERALLS WITH POCKET   *Models 2 and 3*

Pattern pieces: pants front, pants back, shoulder band, pocket, front facing, back facing
Fabric needed: 36″ (90cm) wide: 2⅝yd (2.40m)
               54″ (140cm) wide: 1½yd (1.35m)
Notions: 12″ (30cm) ruched lingerie elastic, snap fasteners

Sewing instructions:

1 Reproduce the pattern pieces on 2 x 2″ (5 x 5cm) dressmaker's pattern paper. Remember to plan for seam allowance. Mark the position of the pocket. Mark where the ruched lingerie elastic is to be stitched on the back panel.

2 With right sides together, fold the fabric in half and pin the pieces to it.

3 Cut out the bottom edge with an extra 1¼″ (3cm) for seam allowance. The remaining edges with an extra ⅜-¾″ (1-2cm) for seam allowance.

4 Zigzag around the edges of the pieces.

5 Stitch the inside leg seams of the pants front and the pants back together.

6 Stitch the middle front and middle back together all the way around. Clip the curve in the seam allowance. Press the seam open. If preferred, iron the seam to one side and stitch it down. In this way the pants get a double row of stitching all the way around, which makes it stronger.

7 Turn in and iron the seam allowance around the pocket. Stitch along the top edge. Stitch the pocket on to the front panel where indicated on the pattern. If desired, at the same time stitch on a loop made of bias binding to the lower corners of the pocket. To make the loops, take a length of bias binding and fold it in half lengthwise. Stitch around the edges and cut to required size. Make into loop and place between pocket and front panel.

8 Stitch ruched lingerie elastic to the back panel where indicated on the pattern.

9 With right sides together, fold the shoulder bands in half and stitch along the edge. Turn them right side out, press and pin them to the back panel.

10 With right sides together, stitch the front facing to the front panel along the top edge and the armholes. Clip the curve in the seam allowance.

11 With right sides together, stitch the back facing to the back panel along the top edge and the armholes. Stitch the shoulder bands on at the same time. Clip the curve of the seam allowance and cut off the corners diagonally.

12 Stitch the side seams together, also the side seams of the front and back facing. Press the seams open.

13 Turn the garment right side out and top-stitch all the way around the top.

14 Sew the lower edge of the facing to the side seams.

15 Turn in the hemlines of the legs and stitch them ¾″ (2cm) from the edge.

16 Attach snap fasteners to the bands and the bib.

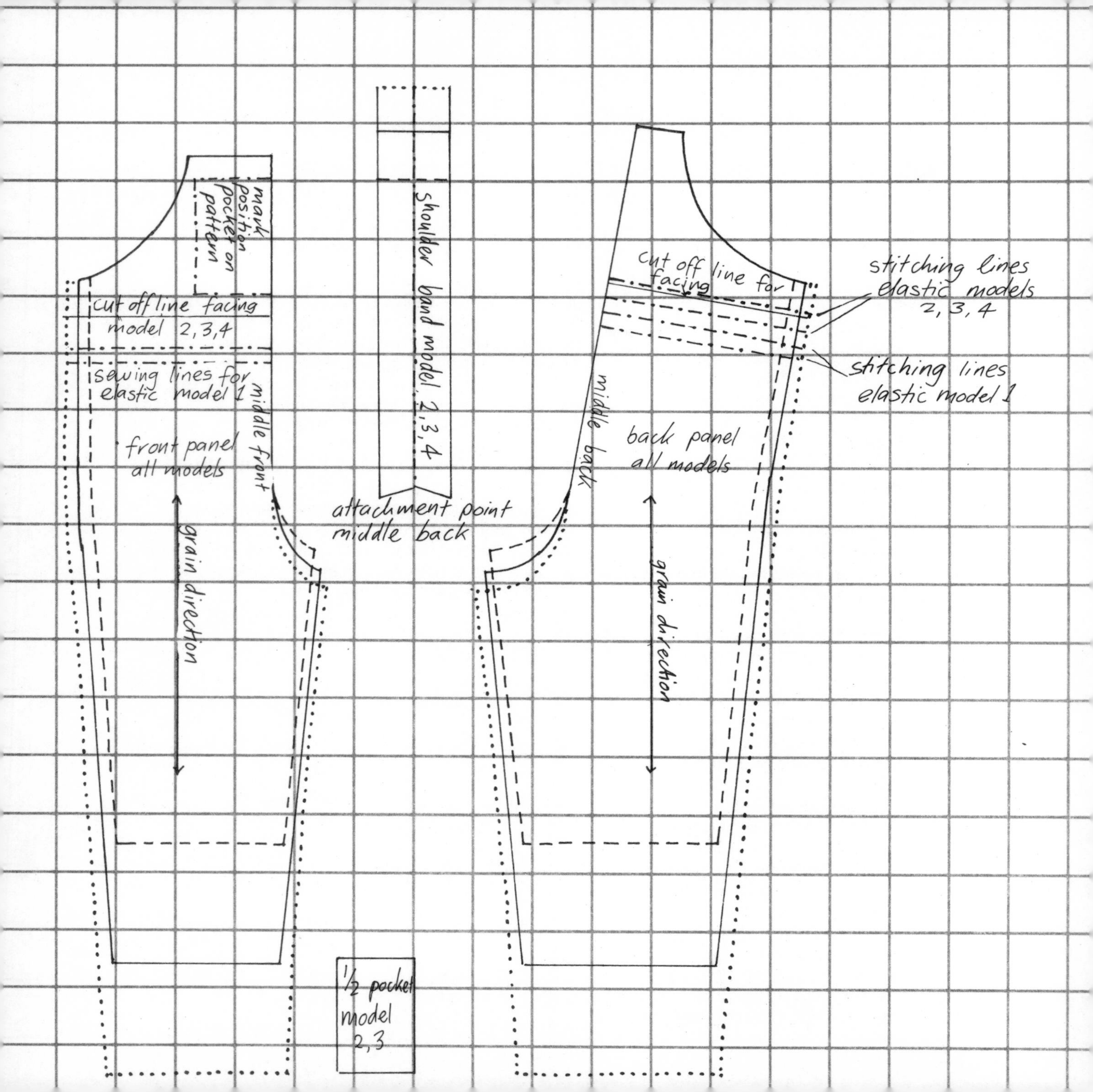

mark position pocket on pattern

cut off line facing model 2,3,4

sewing lines for elastic model 1

front panel all models

middle front

grain direction

Shoulder band model 2,3,4

attachment point middle back

½ pocket model 2,3

cut off line for facing

stitching lines elastic models 2, 3, 4

stitching lines elastic model 1

middle back

back panel all models

grain direction

Jumpsuit, jacket and pants, sleeveless jacket and pants

Fabrics:

Sturdy cottons, like: gabardine, twill, ticking, corduroy, needlecord, velveteen
soft cottons, like: flannelette, poplin.

SLEEVELESS JUMPSUIT   *Model 1*

Size by age: *9-12 mths, 2 years,   4 years*
Height of child: *32" (80cm), 36" (92cm), 40" (104cm)*

Pattern pieces: front panel, back panel, collar, casing, tie belt
Fabric needed: 36" (90cm) wide: 2½yds (2.30m)
54" (140cm) wide: 1½yds (1.35m)
Notions: Zipper: length according to size of garment, 20" (50cm) elastic ⅜" (1cm) wide

Sewing instructions:

1 Reproduce the pattern pieces on 2 x 2" (5 x 5cm) dressmaker's pattern paper. Remember to plan for seam allowance. Mark the position of the casings.
2 With right sides together fold the fabric in half and pin the pieces to it, having the collar and the casing against the fabric fold. Cut out the collar twice. The second time is for the facing. For the tie belt, cut out a strip of fabric measuring 1⅜yd (1.30m) long and 2¼" (6cm) wide.
3 Cut out the middle front with an extra ¾" (2cm) for seam allowance. The bottom edge of the pants legs with an extra 2¾" (7cm) for seam allowance. The remaining edges with an extra ⅜-¾" (1-2cm).
4 Zigzag around the edges of the pieces.

5 Stitch the inside leg seams of the pants front and the pants back together. Press the seams open.
6 Stitch the middle back seam. Place the zipper along the middle front seam ¼" (0.5cm) from the neckline. Mark where the zipper ends. Stitch the middle front seam below this point. Clip the curves in the seam allowance. Press the seam open.
7 Stitch the zipper into the middle front seam. (See p14 for how to insert zipper).
8 Stitch the shoulder seams. Press the seams open.
9 Stitch the side seams. Clip the curves in the seam allowance and press the seams open.
10 Stitch the collar to the neckline. Clip the seam allowance and press it up.
11 With right sides together stitch the facing of the collar to the upper ege of the collar. Clip the curve in the seam allowance. Turn the collar right side out and iron the seam flat. Turn in the lower edge of the collar facing. Stitch to the collar, keeping close to the neckline all the way around.
12 Carrying on from the stitching of the zipper, topstitch all the way around the collar.
13 Turn in the seam allowance of the armholes and stitch down ¼" (0.5cm) from the edge.
14 Turn in and iron the seam allowance of the casing all the way around and stitch on where indicated.
15 Turn in and iron ⅜" (1cm) along the edges of the tie belt all the way around. Fold the belt in half and then stitch all the way around close to the edge.
16 Thread the tie belt through the casing.
17 Turn in 1" (2.5cm) along the bottom edge of the legs. Stitch ½" (1.5cm) from the hemline. Leave a small opening in the seam. Insert the elastic. Stitch both ends of the elastic together and then stitch up the opening.

LONG-SLEEVED JUMPSUIT

Model 2

Size by age: *3 years, 5 years, 7 years*
Height of child: *38″ (98cm), 43″ (110cm), 47″ (122cm)*

Pattern pieces: front panel, back panel, sleeve, collar, casing, tie belt

Fabric needed: 36″ (90cm) wide: 3⅝yds (3.30m)
54″ (140cm) wide: 2¼yds (2.10m)

Notions: Zipper: length according to size of garment, 20″ (50cm) elastic ⅜″ (1cm) wide, 2 D-rings

Sewing instructions:

1 Reproduce the pattern pieces on 2 x 2″ (5 x 5cm) dressmaker's pattern paper. Remember to plan for seam allowance. Mark the position of the casings.

2 With right sides together fold the fabric in half and pin the pieces to it. Pin the collar and the casing against the fabric fold. Cut out the collar twice, the second time for the facing. For the belt, cut out a strip of fabric measuring 1⅜yd (1.30m) long and 2¼″ (6cm) wide.

3 Cut out the middle front with an extra ¾″ (2cm) for seam allowance. The lower edges of the sleeves with an extra 1″ (2.5cm) for seam allowance. The bottom edges of the pants legs with an extra 1¼″ (3cm) for seam allowance. If you want to make baggy pants, cut out the legs 2¾″ (7cm) longer.

4 Zigzag around the edges of the pieces.

5 Stitch the inside leg seams of the pants front and the pants back together. Press the seams open.

6 Stitch the middle back seam. Place the zipper along the middle front seam ¼″ (0.5cm) from the neckline. Mark where the zipper ends and stitch the middle front seam together below this point.

Clip the curves in the seam allowance and press the seam open.

7 Stitch the zipper into the middle front seam. (See p14 for how to insert zipper.)

8 Stitch the side seams. Press the seams open.

9 Stitch the sleeve seams. Press the seams open.

10 Turn the garment so that the right side is on the inside. With right sides together pin the sleeve to the garment, taking care that the front of the raglan section of the sleeve is against the front of the raglan section of the garment. The same applies to the back. Stitch the raglan section all the way around. Clip the curve in the seam allowance and press the seams flat. Turn the garment right side out and topstitch ¼″ (0.5cm) from the seam.

11 Stitch the collar to the neckline. Clip the seam allowance and iron the seam up.

12 With right sides together stitch the upper edge of the facing to the upper edge of the collar. Clip the curve in the seam allowance. Turn the right side out and iron the seam flat. Turn in the bottom edge of the collar facing and stitch it to the collar close to the neckline.

13 Carrying on from the stitching of the zipper, top-stitch all the way around the collar.

14 Turn in 1″ (2.5cm) along the bottom edge of the sleeves and stitch down at ⅝″ (1.5cm) from the edge. Leave a small opening. Insert the elastic into the casing. Stitch the two ends of elastic together and stitch up the opening.

15 Turn in and iron the seam allowances of the casing and stitch on the casing where indicated.

16 Turn in and iron ⅜″ (1cm) all the way around the edge of the belt. Fold it in half, press and stitch it close to the edge all the way around.

17 Thread the tie belt through the casing. Attach the two D rings to one of the ends of the belt.

18 Turn in 1¼" (3cm) along the bottom edges of the legs. Stitch ¾" (2cm) from the bottom edge. If you are making baggy pants, leave a small opening in the seam. Insert the elastic into the opening, stitch the ends together and then stitch up the opening.

JACKET   *Model 3*

Size by age: *3 years,   5 years,   7 years*
Height of child: *38" (98cm), 43" (110cm), 47" (122cm)*

Pattern pieces: front panel, back panel, collar, sleeve
Fabric needed: 36" (90cm) wide: 2⅛yds (1.90m)
                 54" (140cm) wide: 1⅝yds (1.25m)
Notions: 20" (50cm) elastic ⅜" (1cm) wide,
                 1½yds (1.30m) cord, open-ended separating zipper (size required depends on length of middle front seam

Sewing instructions:

1 Reproduce the pattern pieces on 2 x 2" (5 x 5cm) dressmaker's pattern paper. Remember to plan for seam allowance.

2 With right sides together fold the fabric in half and pin the pieces to it, having the back panel and the collar against the fabric fold. The collar is cut out twice. The second time is for the facing.

3 Cut out the middle front with an extra ¾" (2cm) for seam allowance. The bottom edge of the sleeves with an extra 1" (2.5cm) and the bottom edge of the jacket with an extra 1" (2.5cm) for seam allowance. Cut an extra ⅜-¾" (1-2cm) on the remaining edges.

4 Zigzag around the edges of the pieces.

5 Stitch the zipper into the middle front seam, leaving 1½" (4cm) open at the bottom edge. (See p14 for how to insert zipper.)

6 Stitch the side seams. Press the seams open.

7 Stitch the sleeve seams. Press the seams open.

8 Turn the jacket with the right side inside. With right sides together place the sleeve against the jacket. Take care that the front of the raglan section of the sleeve is against the front of the raglan section of the jacket. The same applies to the back. Stitch all the way around the raglan section. Clip the curve in the seam allowance and press the seams flat. Turn the jacket right side out and topstitch along the seam edges.

9 Stitch the collar to the neckline. Clip the seam allowance and iron the seam up.

10 With right sides together stitch the collar facing to the upper edge of the collar. Clip the curve in the seam allowance. Turn the right side out and iron the seam flat. Turn in the lower edge of the collar facing. Stitch it to the collar, close to the neckline.

11 Carrying on from the stitching of the zipper, topstitch all the way around the collar.

12 Turn in 1" (2.5cm) along the bottom of the sleeves and stitch ⅝" (1.5cm) from the bottom edge. Leave a small opening. Thread the elastic through the casing. Stitch the two ends of elastic together and then stitch up the opening.

13 Turn in 1" (2.5cm) along the bottom edge of the jacket. Stitch ⅝" (1.5cm) from the hemline.

14 Thread the cord through the casing.

PANTS

Size by age: *3 years,   5 years,   7 years*
Height of child: *38″ (98cm), 43″ (110cm), 47″ (122cm)*

Pattern pieces: pants front, pants back
Fabric needed: 36″ (90cm) wide: 2¼yds (2.0m)
                54″ (140cm) wide: 1⅛yds (1.0m)
Notions: 1½yds (1.20m) elastic ⅜″ (1cm) wide.
                For baggy pants: 20″ (50cm) extra

Sewing instructions:

1. Reproduce the pattern pieces on 2 x 2″ (5 x 5cm) dressmaker's pattern paper. Remember to plan for seam allowance.
2. With right sides together fold the fabric in half and pin the pieces to it. Cut out the pants with an extra 2″ (5cm) for seam allowance on the upper edge. The bottom edges of the legs need an extra 1″ (2.5cm) for seam allowance. The remaining edges need an extra ⅜-¾″ (1-2cm) for seam allowance. If you intend to make baggy pants, add 2¾″ (7cm) to the length of the legs.
3. Zigzag around the edges of the pieces.
4. Stitch the inside leg seams of the pants front and the pants back together. Press the seams open.
5. Stitch the crotch seams together. Leave 1½″ (4cm) of the seam open at the back. Clip the curve in the seam allowance. Press the seam open.
6. Stitch the side seams. Press the seams open.
7. Turn in 1″ (2.5cm) along the bottom edge of the legs and stitch ¾″ (2cm) from the bottom edge. For baggy pants, leave a small opening and insert the elastic into the opening. Stitch the two ends of elastic together and then stitch up the opening.
8. Turn in 2″ (5cm) along the top edge of the pants. Stitch all the way around ⅜″ (1cm) from the upper edge. Do another row of stitching at 1″ (2.5cm) from the upper edge and then another at 1½″ (4cm) from the upper edge. Insert elastic into the two casings. Stitch the ends of elastic together and then stitch up the openings.

SLEEVELESS JACKET   Model 4

Size by age: *9-12 months, 2 years,   4 years*
Height of child: *31″ (80cm),   36″ (92cm), 40″ (104cm)*

Pattern pieces: front panel, back panel, collar
Fabric needed: 36″ (90cm) wide: 1¼yds (1.10m)
                54″ (140cm) wide: ¾yd (0.60m)
Notions: open-ended separating zipper. The length is dependent upon the width of the knitted cuff.
         knitted cuff for the lower edge of the jacket

Sewing instructions: .

1. Reproduce the pattern pieces on 2 x 2″ (5 x 5cm) dressmaker's pattern paper. Remember to plan for seam allowance.
2. With right sides together fold the fabric in half and pin the pieces to it, having the middle back and the collar against the fabric fold. The collar is cut out twice, the second time is for the facing.
3. Cut out the middle front with an extra ¾″ (2cm) for seam allowance. The rest with an extra ⅜-¾″ (1-2cm) for seam allowance.
4. Zigzag around the edges of the pieces.
5. Stitch the side seams. Clip the curve in the seam allowance and press the seams open.

6 Stitch the knitted cuff to the lower edge.
7 Stitch the zipper into the middle front seam. (See p14 for how to insert zipper).
8 Stitch the shoulder seams and press them open.
9 Turn in the seam allowance of the armholes and stitch at ¼" (0.5cm) from the edge.
10 Stitch the collar to the neckline. Clip the seam allowance and press the seam up.
11 With right sides together stitch the upper edge of the collar facing to the collar. Clip the curve in the seam allowance. Turn in the lower edge of the collar facing. Stitch to the collar, close to the neckline.
12 Carrying on from the stitching of the zipper, top-stitch all around the collar.

PANTS

Size by age: 9-12 mths, 2 years, 4 years
Height of child: 31" (80cm), 36" (92cm), 40" (104cm)

Pattern pieces: pants front, pants back
Fabric needed: 36" (90cm) wide: 1⅞yds (1.70m)
54" (140cm) wide: 1yd (0.85m)
Notions: 1½yds (1.20m) elastic ⅜" (1cm) wide. For baggy pants: 20" (50cm) extra. If desired, 2 knitted cuffs for the ends of the legs.

Sewing instructions:
Follow the instructions for the model 3 pants. If preferred, you can attach knitted cuffs to the legs. If you do, cut the pants slightly shorter, and gather the edges to fit the knitted cuff.

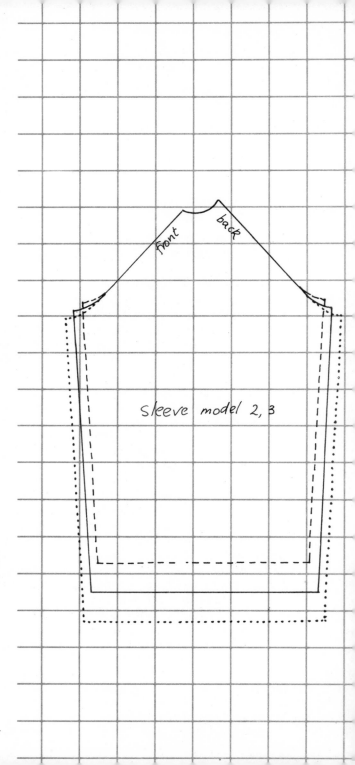
Sleeve model 2, 3
front
back

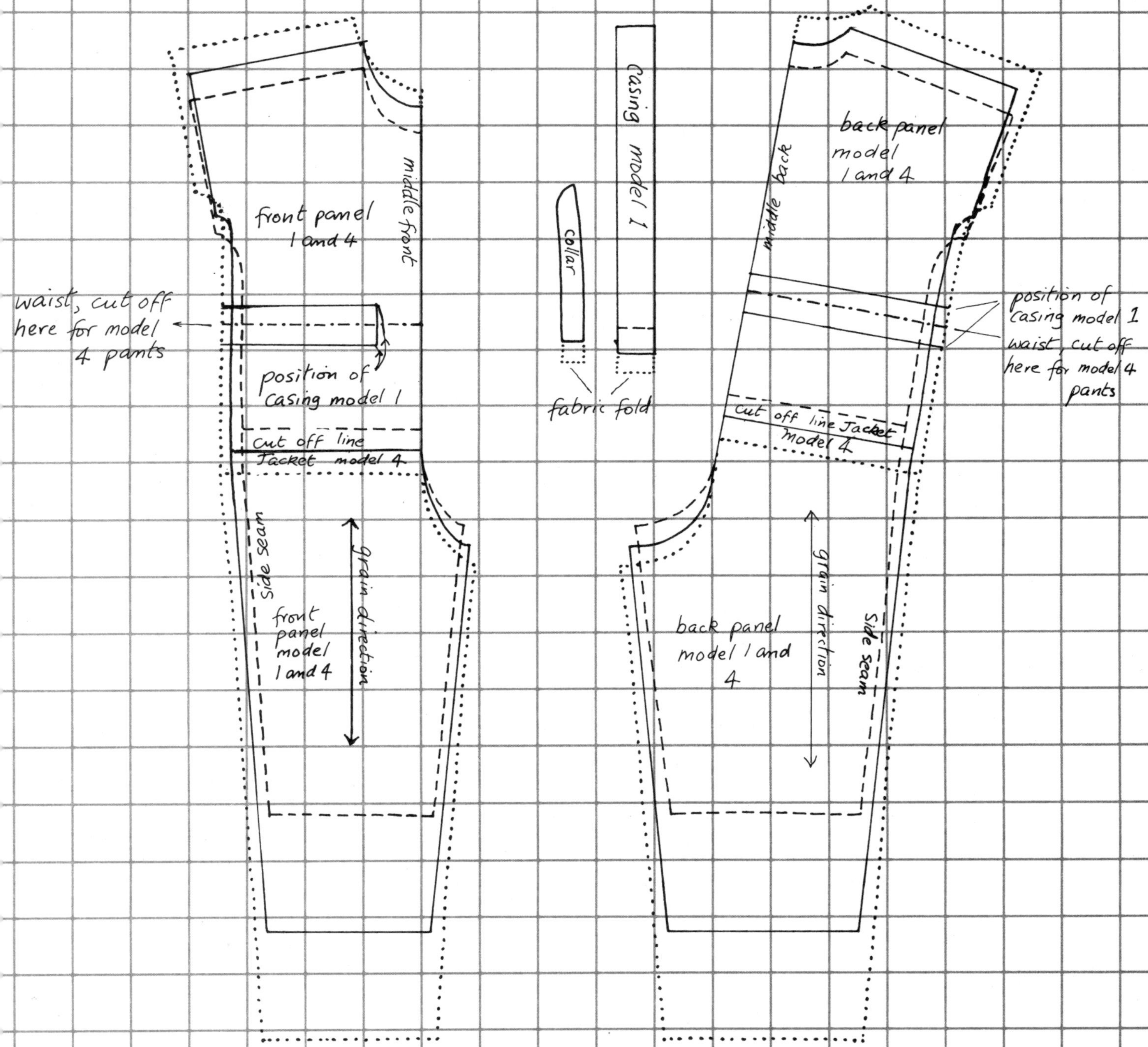

front panel
1 and 4

middle front

waist, cut off
here for model
4 pants

position of
Casing model 1

Cut off line
Jacket model 4

side seam

grain direction

front panel
model
1 and 4

casing model 1

collar

fabric fold

middle back

back panel
model
1 and 4

position of
Casing model 1

waist, cut off
here for model 4
pants

cut off line Jacket
Model 4

grain direction

Side seam

back panel
model 1 and
4

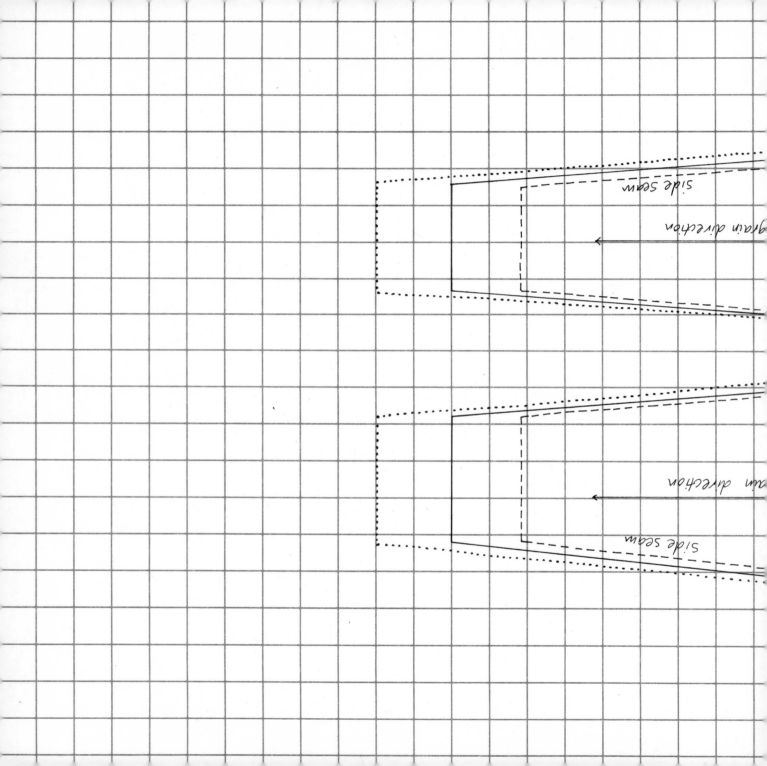

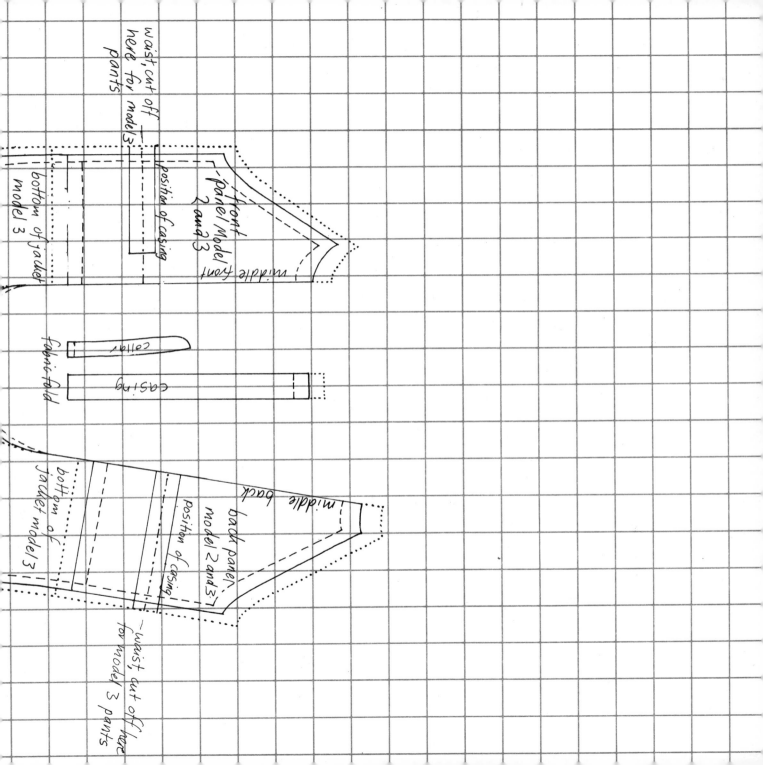

waist, cut off
here for model 3
pants

bottom of jacket
model 3

position of casing

front
panel model
2 and 3

middle front

fabric fold

collar

casing

middle back

back panel
model 2 and 3

position of casing

bottom of
jacket model 3

waist, cut off here
for model 3 pants

3

See P120

117

Pinafores and overalls

Size by age: *18 months, 3 years, 5 years*
Height of child: *34" (86cm), 38" (98cm), 43" (110cm)*
Fabrics: *Denim, twill, poplin, seersucker, flannel, cotton, jacquard, corduroy, velvet.*

PINAFORE   Model 1

Pattern pieces: skirt, bib, waistband, shoulder band
Fabric needed: 36" (90cm) wide: 1⅞yds (1.70m)
54" (140cm) wide: 1¼yds (1.15m)

Sewing instructions:

1 Reproduce the pattern pieces on 2 x 2" (5 x 5cm) dressmaker's pattern paper. Remember to plan for seam allowance. Mark on the waistband where the skirt and the bib are to be attached and the position of the opening.
2 With right sides together fold the fabric in half and pin the pieces to it. If the fabric is 36" (90cm) wide, the middle back and middle front of the skirt, the bib and the waistband are placed against the fold. Cut out the waistband and the bib four times.
3 Cut out the pattern pieces with an extra ⅜-¾" (1-2cm) for seam allowance.
4 Zigzag around the edges of the pieces.
5 Stitch the sides of the skirt together as far as the mark for the opening. Press the seams open. Turn in and stitch the sides of the openings.
6 Gather the top of the skirt until it is the same width as the waistband.
7 Stitch the waistband to the skirt.
8 With right sides together fold the shoulder bands in half and stitch close to the edge. Turn them right side out and press.
9 Stitch the front panel of the bib to the front facing and the back panel of the bib to the back facing.

Do not stitch the bottom edge. At the same time, stitch on the shoulder bands placing them in between the two layers of the bib front and back. Cut off the corners of the seam and turn the bibs right side out. Iron the front, back and shoulder bands and top-stitch them along the edges.
10 Stitch the front bib to the front waistband and the back bib to the back waistband where indicated.
11 Turn in and iron the seam allowance around both waistbands and the waistband facings.
12 Baste the front waistband to the front waistband facing and then stitch it, keeping close to the edge.
13 Baste the back waistband to the back waistband facing and then stitch it, keeping close to the edge.
14 Turn up and stitch the hemline of the skirt.

OVERALLS WITH APPLIQUE   Model 3

Pattern pieces: pants front, pants back, waistband, bib, shoulder band
Fabric needed: 36" (90cm) wide: 2½yds (2.25m)
54" (140cm) wide: 1⅝yds (1.45m)
Notions: scraps of material for applique, two metal clasps

Sewing instructions:

1 Reproduce the pattern pieces on 2 x 2" (5 x 5cm) dressmaker's pattern paper. Remember to plan for seam allowance. Mark the position of the bib and the pants on the waistband. Mark the opening.
2 With right sides together fold the fabric in half and pin the pieces to it, having the bib and the waistband against the fabric fold.
3 Cut out the bib twice and the waistband four times. Cut out the pattern pieces with an extra ⅜-¾" (1-2cm) for seam allowance. Cut out the pants legs with an extra 1¼" (3cm) for seam allowance.

4 Zigzag around the edges of the pieces.
5 Stitch the inside leg seams of the pants front and the pants back together.
6 Reproduce the applique on 2 x 2″ (5 x 5cm) dressmaker's pattern paper. Cut out the pieces in different fabrics, but don't use thick material. Apply fusible webbing to the back of the pieces. Pin to the front of the bib and zigzag in place.
7 Stitch the crotch seam together. Clip the curve in the seam allowance and press the seam open.
8 Stitch the side seams together as far as the mark for the opening. Press the seams open and stitch along the sides of the openings.
9 Gather the top of the pants front and back until they are the same width as the waistband.
10 Stitch the waistband on to the pants.
11 With right sides together fold the shoulder bands in half and stitch along the edge. Turn them right side out and iron. Top-stitch all the way around.
12 Stitch the bibs together. Do not stitch the bottom edge. Cut off the corners of the seam edges diagonally and turn the right side out. Stitch all the way around.
13 Stitch the front of the bib on to the front waistband where indicated on the pattern.
14 Stitch the shoulder bands to the back waistband. Ensure that they can be crossed.
15 Turn in and iron the seam allowance around the front and back waistband and waistband facings.
16 Baste the front waistband to the front waistband facing and stitch them together around the edge.
17 Baste the back waistband to the back waistband facing and stitch them together around the edge.
18 Turn in the hemline of the legs and stitch ¾″ (2cm) from the edge.

PATCHWORK PINAFORE *Model 2* 119

Pattern pieces: skirt, bib, waistband, shoulder band
Fabric needed: all sorts of scraps of fabric
Cut the scraps into squares or rectangles, zigzag around the edges and then stitch them together to make large pieces of fabric. Cut the pattern pieces out of these larger pieces of fabric.
Notions: 2 buttons

Sewing instructions:
Follow the instructions for model 1. The only variations are in steps 2 and 9.

2 With right sides together fold the fabric in half and pin the pieces to it. Cut out the bib twice against the fabric fold and twice *not* against the fabric fold. The waistband is also placed against the fold. Cut out the waistband four times.
9 Stitch the bibs together. With right sides together, stitch the front facing to the front panel, and the two back facings to the two back panels. At the same time, stitch on the shoulder bands between the two layers of fabric on the upper edge. Also stitch on two loops close to the top of the middle back seam of one of the back sections of the bib. Make the loops and place between the two layers of fabric. To make the loops, measure the amount of bias binding needed for each button. Fold the binding in half lengthwise and stitch around the edges. Cut off the corners of the seam edges diagonally and turn the sections right side out. Sew two buttons on to the back, opposite the loops.

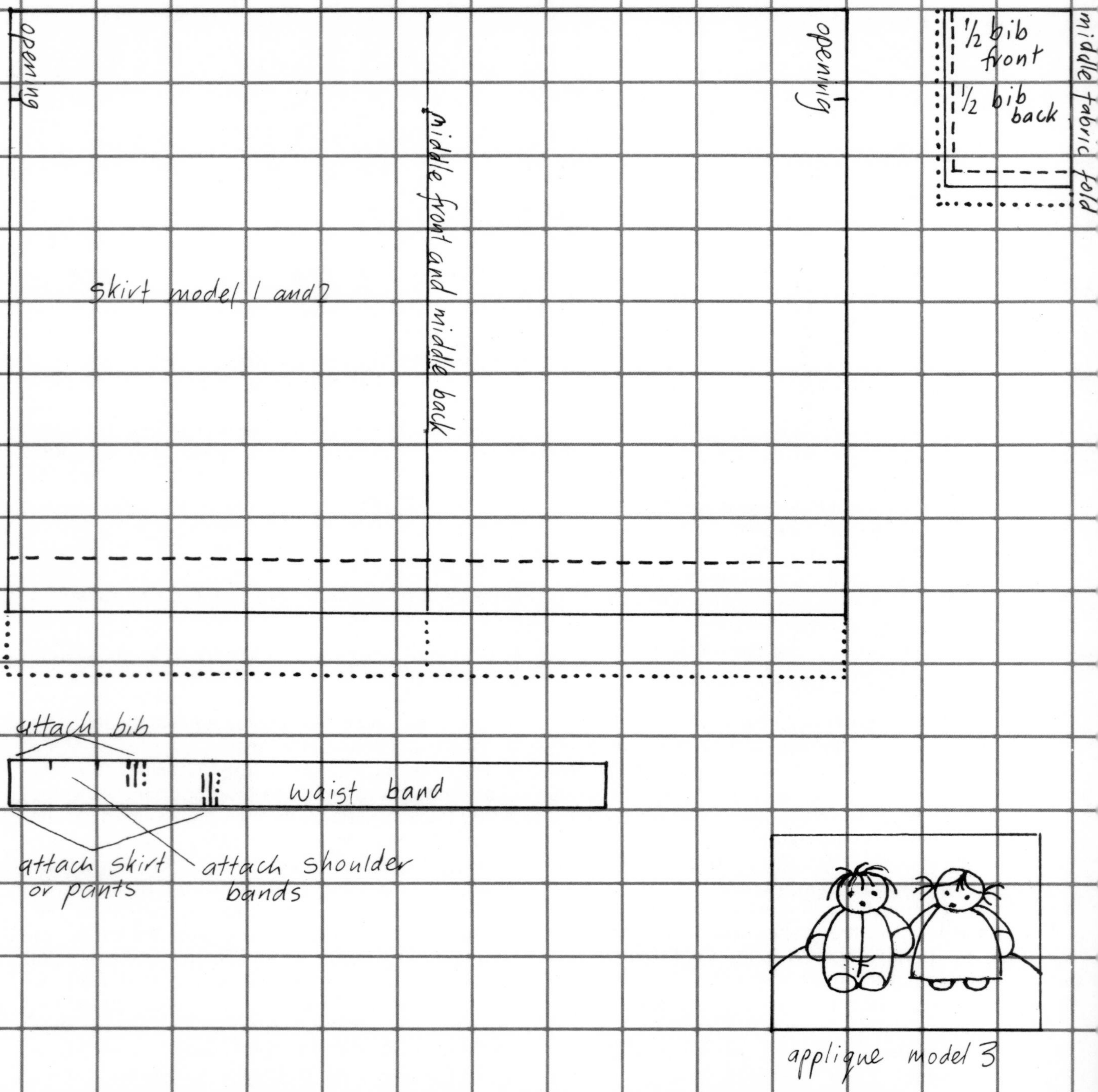

opening

opening

middle fabric fold

½ bib front

½ bib back

middle front and middle back

skirt model 1 and 2

attach bib

waist band

attach skirt or pants

attach shoulder bands

applique model 3

120

see p 117

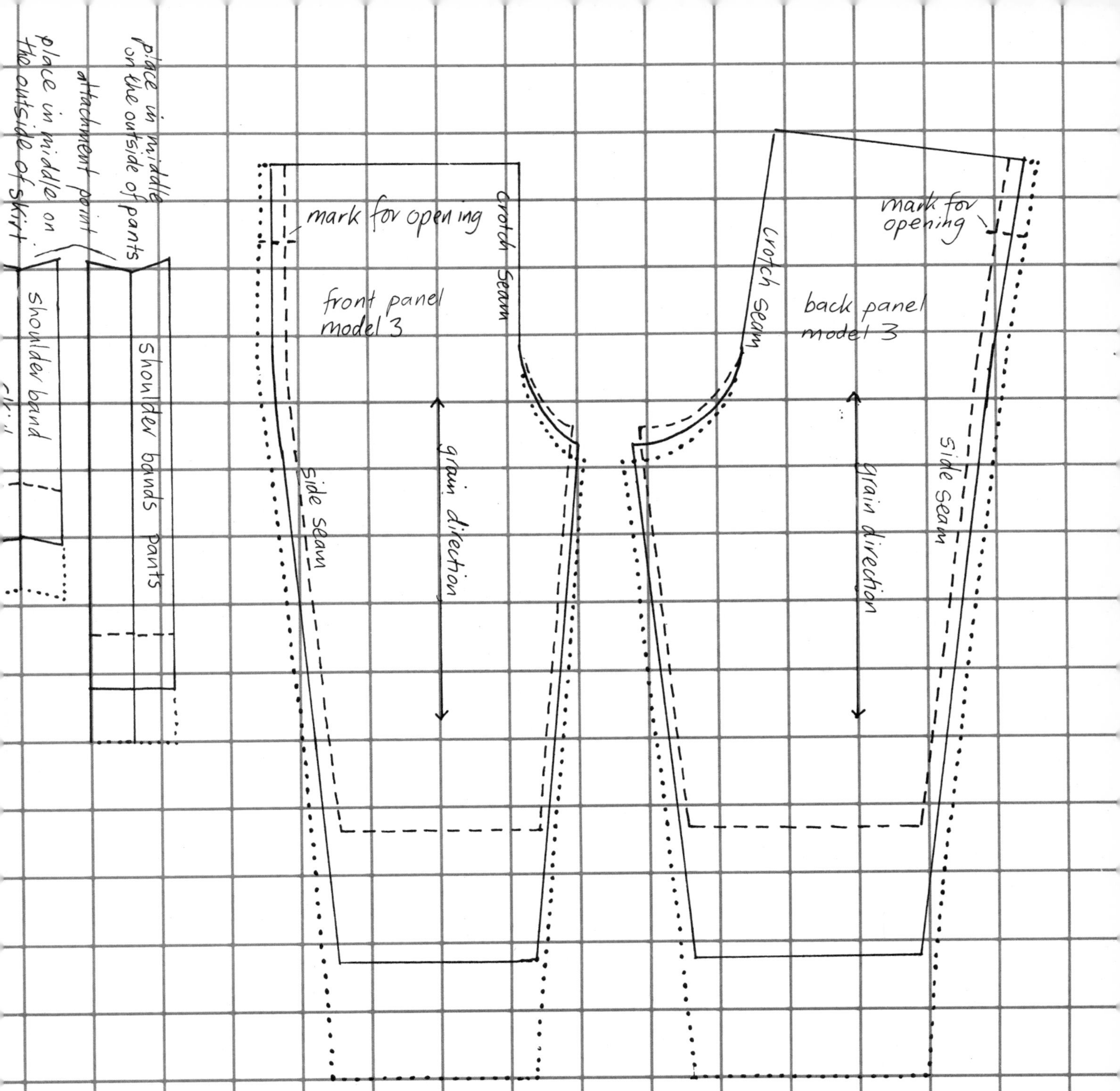

place in middle on the outside of pants

attachment point

place in middle on the outside of skirt

shoulder band

Shoulder bands pants

mark for opening

Crotch Seam

front panel model 3

side seam

grain direction

mark for opening

Crotch seam

back panel model 3

grain direction

Side Seam

1   2   3

See P.127

4

5

Dresses

Size by age: *2 years, 4 years, 6 years*
Height of child: *36" (92cm), 40" (104cm), 45" (116cm)*
Fabrics: *All sorts of soft fabrics such as: poplin, embroidered cotton, flannel, seersucker, velvet, corduroy, glazed cotton, viyella.*

PINAFORE WITH FRILLS   Model 1

Pattern pieces: skirt front, skirt back, front panel bib, back panel bib, frill
Fabric needed: 36" (90cm) wide: 1¾yds (1.65m)
54" (140cm) wide: 1⅛yds (1.0m)
Notions: 12" (30cm) zipper

Sewing instructions:

1 Reproduce the pattern pieces on 2 x 2" (5 x 5cm) dressmaker's pattern paper. Remember to plan for seam allowance.
2 With right sides together fold the fabric in half and pin the pieces to it, having the middle front of the bib, middle front of the skirt and the frill against the fold. The bib is cut out twice. The second time is for the facing. For the facing, the middle front is also placed against the fabric fold. The frill is also cut out twice, each time against the fabric fold.
3 Cut the outer edge of the frill with an extra ¼" (0.5cm) for seam allowance. Cut out the remaining edges with an extra ⅜-¾" (1-2cm).
4 Zigzag around the edges of the pieces.
5 Stitch the middle back seam of the skirt as far as the mark for the opening. Stitch the side seams of the skirt together. Press the seams open.
6 Gather the top of the skirt until it is the same width as the bib.
7 Turn in and stitch ¼" (0.5cm) along the outer edge of both frills. Gather them until they measure 8½" (22cm).
8 Stitch the shoulder seams together, press them open.
9 Baste the frills to the bib, having the middle of the frill against the shoulder seam.
10 Stitch the shoulder seams of the bib facings together.
11 With right sides together, stitch the bib and bib facings together around the neckline and both armholes. At the same time, stitch on the frill. Make sure that the frill is on the right side when you turn the garment the right way round. Clip the curves in the seam allowance. Turn the right side out and press the seams flat.
12 Stitch the side seams of the bib and facing.
13 Stitch the skirt to the bib.
14 Turn in and iron the seam allowance of the bib and the facing. Stitch the zipper into the back seam. (See p14 for how to insert zipper.) Stitch the top part of the zipper between the back section of the bib and the back facing of the bib.
15 Top-stitch around the bib just above the waistline. At the same time, top-stitch along the middle back edges and around the neckline and armholes, keeping close to the edge.
16 Turn in and stitch the hemline of the skirt.

SLEEVELESS DRESS WITH APPLIQUE   Model 2

Pattern pieces: skirt front, skirt back, front bodice panel, back bodice panel, pocket
Fabric needed: 36" (90cm) wide: 2⅛yds (1.90m)
54" (140cm) wide: 1yd (0.95m)

Notions: 12″ (30cm) zipper, 32″ (80cm) bias
binding, scraps of fabric for appliqué

Sewing instructions:

1. Reproduce the pattern pieces on 2 x 2″ (5 x 5cm)
dressmaker's pattern paper. Remember to plan for
seam allowance and mark the position for the pockets.
2. With right sides together fold the fabric in half and
pin the pieces to it, having the middle front of the
bodice and middle front of the skirt on the fold.
3. Cut out the neckline and the armholes without a
seam allowance. Cut out the remaining edges with
an extra ⅜-¾″ (1-2cm) for seam allowance.
4. Zigzag around the edges of the pieces.
5. Reproduce the drawing of the applique on 2 x 2″
(5 x 5cm) dressmaker's pattern paper. Cut out the
various sections in fabric without any seam allowance. Don't use very thick fabric. Apply fusible webbing to the backs of the fabric pieces. Pin the
applique to the bodice and zigzag around the
edges.
6. Stitch the middle back seam of the skirt as far as
the mark for the opening. Stitch the side seams of
the skirt. Press the seams open. Turn in and iron
the seam allowance around the pockets. Stitch
along the top edge and then stitch the pockets on
where indicated.
7. Gather the top of the skirt until it is the same width
as the bodice.
8. Stitch the shoulder seams together. Press them
open. Stitch bias binding around the armholes.
9. Stitch the underarm seams of the bodice together.
Clip the curve in the seam allowance and press
the seams open.

10. Stitch the skirt to the bodice. Press the seam up
and top-stitch just above the waistline.
11. Stitch the zipper into the middle back seam.
12. Stitch bias binding around the neckline.
13. Turn in and stitch the hemline of the skirt.

LONG-SLEEVED DRESS   *Model 3*

Pattern pieces: skirt front, skirt back, front bodice
panel, back bodice panel, front facing,
back facing
Fabric needed: 54″ (140cm) wide: 1¾yds (1.60m)
Notions: 12″ (30cm) zipper,
20″ (50cm) elastic ⅜″ (1cm) wide

Sewing instructions:

Follow the instructions for model 2. The only variations
are in steps 1,2,3,8 and 12. Step 5 is omitted. Step 14
is added.

1. Reproduce the pattern pieces on 2 x 2″ (5 x 5cm)
dressmaker's pattern paper. Remember to plan for
seam allowance. Join the shoulder seams of the
front facing and back facing together and cut out
as one piece.
2. With right sides together fold the fabric in half and
pin the pieces to it, having the middle front of the
bodice, the neckline facing and the skirt against
the fabric fold.
3. Cut out all seams with an extra ⅜-¾″ (1-2cm) for
seam allowance. The bottom edge of the sleeves
has an extra 1″ (2.5cm) for seam allowance.
8. Stitch the shoulder seams and press them open.
12. With right sides together, stitch the facing to the
neckline then turn it right side out and sew the
middle back to the zipper.

14 Turn in 1″ (2.5cm) along the bottom edge of the sleeves and stitch ⅝″ (1.5cm) from the edge. Leave a small opening. Insert the elastic. Stitch the two ends of the elastic together and then stitch up the opening.

SUNDRESS   *Model 4*

Pattern pieces: skirt front, skirt back, front bib panel, back bib panel
Fabric needed: 36″ (90cm) wide: 1¾yds (1.65m)
54″ (140cm) wide: 1⅛yds (1.0m)

Sewing instructions:

1 Reproduce the pattern pieces on 2 x 2″ (5 x 5cm) dressmaker's pattern paper. Remember to plan for seam allowance.
2 With right sides together fold the fabric in half and pin the pieces to it, having the middle front and middle back of the skirt, middle front and middle back of the bib against the fold. The front panel of the bib and the back panel of the bib are cut out twice, both times against the fold. The second time is for the facing.
3 Cut out the seams with an extra ⅜-¾″ (1-2cm) for seam allowance. Cut out two straight strips 2¾″ (7cm) long and 1½″ (4cm) wide. Zigzag around the edges of the pieces.
4 Stitch the side seams of the skirt. Press the seams open.
5 Gather the top of the skirt until it is the same width as the bib.
6 Stitch the side seams of the bib and bib facings. Press the seams open.

7 Turn in and iron ⅜″ (1cm) along the edges of the shoulder straps all the way around. Fold them in half lengthwise and stitch along the edge.
8 Pin the shoulder straps to the front panel and two loops on the back panel where indicated on the pattern. To make the loops, fold a piece of bias binding in half and stitch around the edges. Form into loop. Stitch the bib and the facing together all the way around, stitching the straps and loops on at the same time. Do not stitch the bottom edge.
9 Clip the curve in the seam allowance. Turn the right side out and press the seams flat.
10 Stitch the skirt to the bib. Press the seam up. Topstitch just above the waistline.
11 Turn in and stitch the hemline of the skirt.

PINAFORE   *Model 5*

Pattern pieces: skirt front, skirt back, front bodice panel, back bodice panel
Fabric needed: 36″ (90cm) wide: 1¾yd (1.55m)
54″ (140cm) wide: 1yd (0.95m)
Notions: 12″ (30cm) zipper

Sewing instructions:
Follow the instructions for model 1. Omit everything referring to the frills.

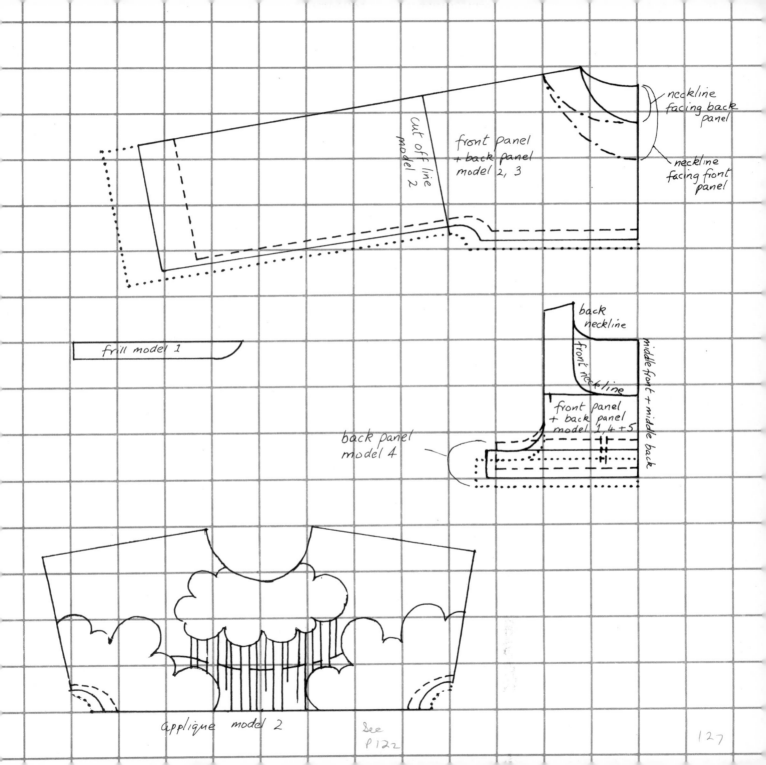

neckline facing back panel

neckline facing front panel

cut off line model 2

front panel + back panel model 2, 3

back neckline

front neckline

middle front + middle back

front panel + back panel model 1, 4 + 5

frill model 1

back panel model 4

appliqué model 2

See P 122

127

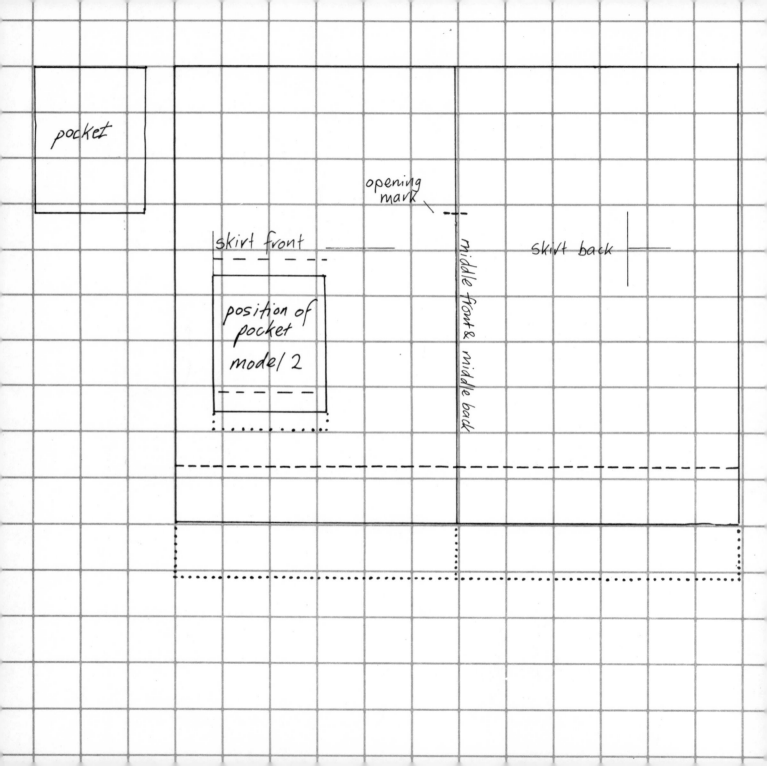

pocket

skirt front

opening mark

middle front & middle back

skirt back

position of
pocket
model 2

3

4

5

6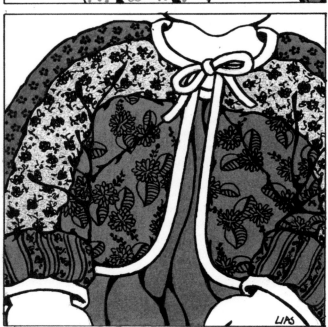

All kinds of jackets

Size by age: *2 years,   4 years,   6 years*
Height of child: *36″ (92cm), 40″ (104cm), 45″ (116cm)*
Fabrics: *Printed cotton, plain cotton, flannel, corduroy, velvet, quilted cotton, jacquard, jacquard lined with acrylic fur, velvet lined with flannel, glazed cotton lined with corduroy, optional: wadding in between the two layers.*

JACKET WITH CROCHETED SEAMS   Model 1

Pattern pieces: front panel, back panel
Fabric needed: 54″ (140cm) wide knitted fabric:
⅞yd (0.80m)
Notions: 3¼yd (3.0m) bias binding, remnants of wool or cotton yarn, crochet hook

Sewing instructions:

1 Reproduce the pattern pieces on 2 x 2″ (5 x 5cm) dressmaker's pattern paper.
2 With right sides together fold the fabric in half and pin the pieces to it, having the middle back against the fabric fold.
3 Cut out all the pieces without a seam allowance.
4 Zigzag around the edges of each piece.
5 Crochet the underarm side seams together.
6 Crochet the upper arm seams together.
7 Stitch bias binding around the bottom edge of the sleeves.
8 Stitch bias binding all around the edge of the jacket. At the same time stitch a bias binding tie halfway down each side of the opening. To make the ties, cut two 12″ (30cm) lengths of bias binding. Fold in half lengthwise and stitch around the edges.

KNITTED JACKET   Model 2

Pattern pieces: front panel, back panel
Notions: knitting yarn, knitting needles, crochet hook

Instructions:

1 Reproduce the pattern pieces on 2 x 2″ (5 x 5cm) dressmaker's pattern paper.
2 Fold a piece of paper in half and lay the pieces on it, having the middle back and middle front against the fold. Cut out without a seam allowance.
3 Knit the model in a plain stitch to match the pattern pieces. Knit the front panel twice, remembering to knit the second one the opposite way around to the first.
4 Sew the seams together.
5 Crochet loops to the edge of the wrapover. These are for the buttons. Also crochet a loop on the inside flap to prevent this hanging down.
6 Sew the buttons on to the front panels.

You can also cut this pattern out of an old pullover or a length of tricot fabric.

SLEEVELESS BOLERO JACKET   Model 3

Pattern pieces: front panel, back panel
Fabric needed: 36″ (90cm) wide: ¾yd (0.70m)
54″ (140cm) wide: ⅜yd (0.35m)
or sew strips of fabric together to make one large piece
Notions: 2½yd (2.30m) bias binding

Sewing instructions:

1 Reproduce the pattern pieces on 2 x 2" (5 x 5cm) dressmaker's pattern paper. Remember to plan for seam allowance.
2 With right sides together fold the fabric in half and pin the pieces to it, having the middle back against the fabric fold.
3 Cut out the shoulder seams and the side seams with an extra ⅜-¾" (1-2cm) for seam allowance. The remaining edges without a seam allowance.
4 Stitch the shoulder seams. Press the seams open.
5 Stitch the side seams together. Clip the curves in the seam allowance and press the seams open.
6 Stitch bias binding around the armholes.
7 Stitch bias binding all around the edge of the garment.

LINED JACKET   *Model 4*

Pattern pieces: front panel, back panel
Fabric needed: 54" (140cm) wide: 1yd (0.85m)
Lining fabric: 54" (140cm) wide: 1yd (0.85m)
Notions: 10" (25cm) bias binding, 3 buttons

Sewing instructions:

1 Reproduce the pattern pieces on 2 x 2" (5 x 5cm) dressmaker's pattern paper. Remember to plan for seam allowance.
2 With right sides together fold the fabric in half and pin the pieces to it, having the middle back against the fabric fold.
3 Cut out the pieces with an extra ⅜-¾" (1-2cm) for seam allowance.

4 Fold the lining fabric in half and pin the pattern pieces to it, having the middle back against the fabric fold. Cut out the pieces with an extra ⅜-¾" (1-2cm) for seam allowance.
5 Zigzag around the edges of the pieces.
6 Stitch the underarm side seams of the jacket together. Stitch the upper arm seams of the jacket together. Clip the curves in the seam allowance. Press the seams open. Repeat this step with the lining fabric.
7 With right sides together, fit the two jackets into each other.
8 Stitch the lining and the outer jacket together. At the same time, stitch on three loops to one of the middle front edges. To make the loops, measure the amount of bias binding needed for each button. Cut a length long enough for 3 loops. Fold in half and stitch around the edges. Cut into three pieces and form into loops. Leave the bottom edge open. Stitch the bottom edges of the sleeves together. Cut off the corners of the neckline seam edges diagonally and turn the jacket right side out.
9 Turn in the bottom edges of the lining and outer jacket and stitch these together.
10 Top-stitch all the way around the jacket. Top-stitch around the ends of the sleeves.

SLEEVELESS JACKET WITH TIE FASTENING
Model 5

Pattern pieces: front panel, back panel
Fabric needed: 36" (90cm) wide: ¾yd (0.70m)
                 54" (140cm) wide: ⅜yd (0.35m)
Notions: 3⅜yd (3.10m) bias binding

Sewing instructions:

Follow the instructions for model 3. The only variation is in step 7.

7 Stitch bias binding around the edge of the jacket. Stitch bias binding around the neckline. Allow 24" (60cm) more bias binding than you need and leave 12" (30cm) loose on each side for the ties.

JACKET   *Model 6*

Pattern pieces: front panel, back panel
Fabric needed: 54" (140cm) wide: 1yd (0.85m)
or sew strips of fabric together as indicated on the pattern. Zigzag the edges of the strips before stitching them together. If making this jacket with wadding between the outer fabric and the lining, then the seams must be quilted

Sewing instructions:

Follow the instructions for model 3. The only variations are in steps 6 and 7.

6 Finish the ends of the sleeves with bias binding.
7 Finish the edges of the jacket with bias binding. Stitch bias binding around the neckline. Allow 24" (60cm) more bias binding than you need for the neckline and leave 12" (30cm) loose on both sides.

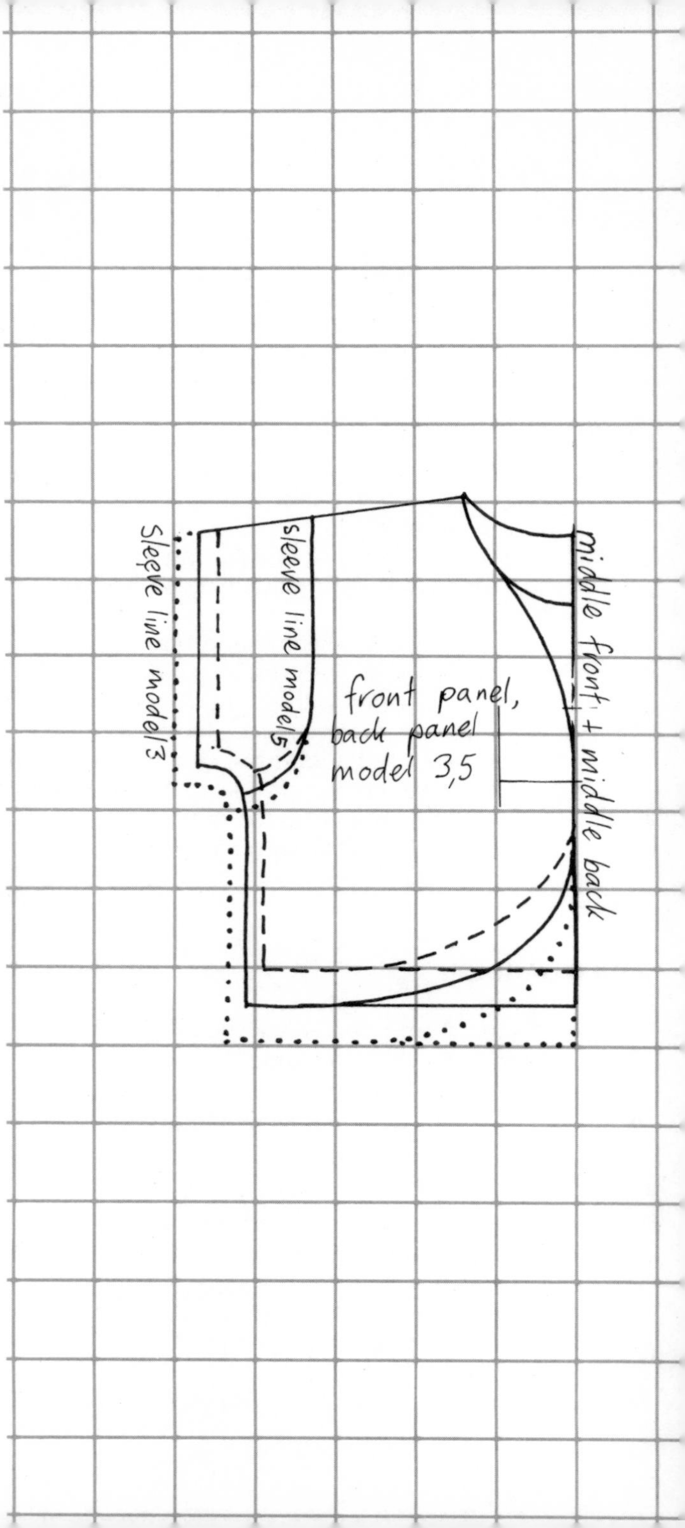

sleeve line model 3

sleeve line model 5

front panel, back panel model 3,5

middle front + middle back

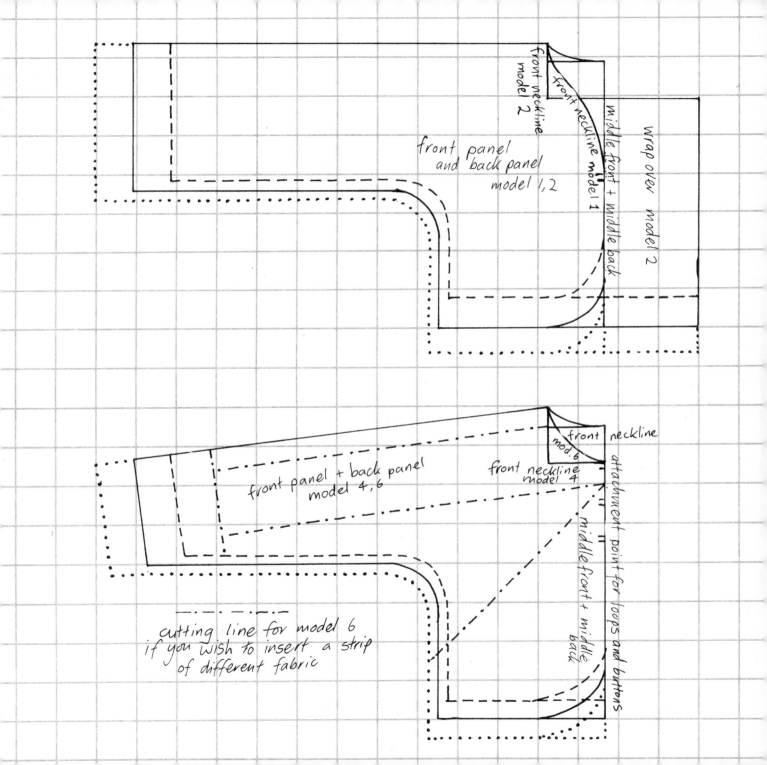

front neckline model 2

front neckline model 1

middle front + middle back

wrap over model 2

front panel
and back panel
model 1, 2

front neckline

front neckline
model 4

mod. 6

front panel + back panel
model 4, 6

middle front + middle back

attachment point for loops and buttons

cutting line for model 6
if you wish to insert a strip
of different fabric

137

All kinds of Dresses

Size by age: *3 years,   5 years,   7 years*
Height of child: *38" (98cm), 43" (110cm), 47" (122cm)*
Fabrics: *Soft fabrics such as: printed cotton, poplin, batiste, embroidered cotton, crepe, seersucker, viyella.*

DRESS WITH FRILLS   Model 1

Pattern pieces: front panel, back panel, sleeve, frill
Fabric needed: 36" (90cm) wide: 3⅞yd (3.50m)
54" (140cm) wide: 2⅞yd (2.70m)
Notions: 12" (30cm) zipper,
16" (40cm) bias binding,
18" (45cm) elastic ⅜" (1cm) wide

Sewing instructions:

1 Reproduce the pattern pieces on 2 x 2" (5 x 5cm) dressmaker's pattern paper. Remember to plan for seam allowance. Mark which is the front and the back section on the sleeve and the frill.
2 With right sides together fold the fabric in half and pin the pieces to it, having the middle of the front panel against the fabric fold.
3 Cut out the bottom edge of the sleeve with an extra 1" (2.5cm) for seam allowance. Cut out the neckline, the neckline edge of the sleeve and the neckline side of the frill without a seam allowance. The outside edge of the frill has an extra ¼" (0.5cm) for seam allowance. The remaining edges need an extra ⅜-¾" (1-2cm) for seam allowance.
4 Zigzag around the edges of the pieces.
5 Stitch the middle back seam stopping 12" (30cm) from the neckline. Press the seam open.
6 Stitch the zipper into the middle back opening. (See p14 for instructions on how to insert zipper.)
7 Stitch the side seams together and press them open.
8 Stitch the sleeve seams together and press them open.
9 Turn in the outer edges of the frills, stitch them down and pin the frills to the neckline of the sleeve.
10 Stitch the sleeves into the armholes, stitching the sides of the frills at the same time. See that the front of the raglan section of the sleeve is against the raglan section of the front panel. Clip the curve in the seam allowance and press the seams open.
11 Gather the neckline of the dress until it measures 12" (31cm), 13" (33cm) or 14" (35cm) according to size. Gather the frills at the same time.
12 Stitch bias binding around the neckline.
13 Turn in the bottom edge of the sleeves and stitch ⅝" (1.5cm) from the bottom edge. Leave a small opening and thread elastic through the casing. Stitch the two ends of the elastic together and then stitch up the opening.
14 Turn in the hemline of the dress and stitch.

DRESS WITH APPLIQUED YOKE   Model 2

Pattern pieces: front panel, back panel, sleeve, front yoke, back yoke
Fabric needed: 36" (90cm) wide: 3¾yd (3.40m)
54" (140cm) wide: 2⅞yd (2.65m)
Notions: 16" (40cm) bias binding,
½yd (45cm) elastic ⅜ (1cm) wide,
12" (30cm) zipper,
scraps of fabric for applique
Applique: Cut out the separate pieces in fabric without a seam allowance. Apply fusible webbing to the back of the pieces.

Pin the pieces to the front yoke and zigzag in place around the edges. Do this before the dress is stitched together.

Sewing instructions:

1 Reproduce the pattern pieces on 2 x 2″ (5 x 5cm) dressmaker's pattern paper. Remember to plan for seam allowance. Mark which is the front and which is the back on the sleeve.
2 With right sides together fold the fabric in half and pin the pieces to it, having the middle front of the front panel and the yoke against the fabric fold. (If you wish you can cut out the front yoke in a different fabric).
3 Cut out the neckline and the neckline side of the sleeves without a seam allowance. Cut out the bottom edge of the sleeves with an extra 1″ (2.5cm) for seam allowance. The rest with an extra ⅜-¾″ (1-2cm) for seam allowance.
4 Zigzag around the edges of the pieces.
5 Gather the two back panels until they are the same width as the back yoke. Stitch the two back panels to the back yoke. Iron the seam up and top-stitch close to the seam.
6 Stitch the middle back seam, stopping 12″ (30cm) from the neckline. Press the seam open.
7 Stitch the zipper into the back opening. (See p14 for how to insert zipper.)
8 Gather the front panel until it is the same width as the front yoke. Stitch the front panel and the front yoke together. Press the seam up and top-stitch close to the seam.
9 Stitch the side seams and press them open.
10 Stitch the sleeve seams and press them open.
11 Stitch the sleeves to the armholes. See that the front of the raglan section of the sleeve is against the raglan section of the front panel. Clip the curves in the seam and press the seams open.
12 Gather the neckline around the shoulders until each side measures 2¼″ (6cm).
13 Stitch bias binding around the neckline.
14 Turn in the bottom edges of the sleeves and stitch ⅝″ (1.5cm) from the bottom edge. Leave a small opening and thread the elastic through the casing. Stitch the two ends of the elastic together and then stitch up the opening.
15 Turn in and stitch the hemline of the dress.

SUNDRESS WITH YOKE   *Model 3*

Pattern pieces: front panel, back panel, front yoke, back yoke
Fabric needed: 36″ (90cm) wide: 2⅛yd (1.95m)
54″ (140cm) wide: 2⅛yd (1.95m)
Notions: 3¼yd (3.0m) bias binding

Sewing instructions:

1 Reproduce the pattern pieces on 2 x 2″ (5 x 5cm) dressmaker's pattern paper. Remember to plan for seam allowance.
2 With right sides together fold the fabric in half and pin the pieces to it. Place all the pieces against the fabric fold.
3 Cut out the pieces along the neckline and armholes without a seam allowance. The remaining edges with an extra ⅜-¾″ (1-2cm) for seam allowance.
4 Zigzag around the edges of the pieces.
5 Stitch the side seams and press them open.

6   Gather the top of the front panel until it is the same width as the front yoke.
7   Stitch the front yoke to the front panel. Press the seam up and top-stitch close to the seam.
8   Gather the top of the back panel until it is the same width as the back yoke.
9   Stitch the back yoke to the back panel. Press the seam up and top-stitch close to the seam.
10 Stitch bias binding around the armholes.
11 Stitch bias binding around the front neckline. Allow 28" (70cm) more bias binding than needed for the front neckline and leave 14" (35cm) loose on each side.
12 Stitch bias binding around the back neckline. Allow 28" (70cm) more bias binding than needed for the back neckline and leave 14" (35cm) loose on each side.
13 Turn in and stitch the hemline of the skirt.

SUNDRESS OR PINAFORE   Model 4

Pattern pieces: front panel, back panel
Fabric needed: 36" (90cm) wide: 2¼yd (2.0m)
                   54" (140cm) wide: 2¼yd (2.0m)
Notions: 3¼yd (3.0m) bias binding

Sewing instructions:
1   Reproduce the pattern pieces on 2 x 2" (5 x 5cm) dressmaker's pattern paper. Remember to plan for seam allowance.
2   With right sides together fold the fabric in half and pin the pieces to it, having the middle of the front and back panels against the fabric fold.
3   Cut out the pieces along the neckline and armholes without a seam allowance. The remaining edges with an extra ⅜-¾" (1-2cm) for seam allowance.

4   Zigzag around the edges of the pieces.
5   Stitch the side seams together and press them open.
6   Gather the front neckline until it is 6" (14cm) wide.
7   Gather the back neckline until it is 4" (10cm) wide.
8   Stitch bias binding around the armholes.
9   Stitch bias binding around the front neckline. Allow 28" (70cm) more bias binding than you need for the neckline and leave 14" (35cm) loose on each side.
10 Stitch bias binding around the back neckline. Allow 28" (70cm) more bias binding than you need for the back neckline and leave 14" (35cm) loose on each side.

DRESS   Model 5

Pattern pieces: front panel, back panel, sleeve
Fabric needed: 36" (90cm) wide: 3¾yd (3.40m)
                   54" (140cm) wide: 3yd (2.70m)
Notions: 16" (40cm) bias binding, 18" (45cm) elastic (1cm) wide, 12" (30cm) zipper

Sewing instructions:
1   Reproduce the pattern pieces on 2 x 2" (5 x 5cm) dressmaker's pattern paper. Remember to plan for seam allowance. Mark the sleeves to indicate which side is the front and which side is the back.
2   With right sides together fold the fabric in half and pin the pieces to it, having the middle of the front panel against the fabric fold.
3   Cut out the pieces along the neckline and neckline edge of the sleeves without a seam allowance. The bottom edge of the sleeves with an extra 1" (2.5cm) for seam allowance. The remaining edges with an extra ⅜-¾" (1-2cm) for seam allowance.

4 Zigzag around the edges of the pieces.
5 Stitch the middle back seam, stopping 12″ (30cm) from the neckline.
6 Stitch the zipper into the middle back opening. (See p14 for how to insert zipper.)
7 Stitch the side seams, press the seams open.
8 Stitch the sleeve seams and press the seams open.
9 Stitch the sleeves into the armholes. See that the front of the raglan section of the sleeve is against the raglan section of the front panel. Clip the curve in the seam allowance and press the seams open.
10 Gather the neckline until it is 12″ (31cm), 13″ (33cm) or 14″ (35cm) wide, according to size.
11 Stitch bias binding around the neckline.
12 Turn in the bottom edge of the sleeves and stitch ½″ (1.5cm) from the edge. Leave a small opening. Thread elastic through the casing. Stitch the two ends of elastic together and then stitch up the opening.
13 Turn in and stitch the hemline of the dress.

PINAFORE   Model 6

Pattern pieces: front panel, back panel, frill
Fabric needed: 36″ (90cm) wide: 2¼yd (2.10m)
       54″ (140cm) wide: 2⅛yd (2.0m)
Notions: 1¾yd (1.60m) bias binding,
       12″ (30cm) zipper

Sewing instructions:

1 Reproduce the pattern pieces on 2 x 2″ (5 x 5cm) dressmaker's pattern paper. Remember to plan for seam allowance. Mark the frill to indicate which side is the front and the back.

2 With right sides together fold the fabric in half and pin the pieces to it, having the middle of the front panel against the fabric fold.
3 Cut out the pieces along the neckline and neckline edge of the sleeves without a seam allowance. The armholes, the sides and the outside of the frill with an extra ¼″ (0.5cm) for seam allowance. The remaining edges with an extra ⅜-¾″ (1-2cm) for seam allowance.
4 Zigzag around the edges of the pieces.
5 Stitch the middle back seam, stopping 12″ (30cm) from the neckline. Press the seam open.
6 Stitch the zipper into the back opening. (See p14 for how to insert zipper.)
7 Stitch the side seams and press them open.
8 Turn in and stitch the outer edge of the frill.
9 Pin the sides of the frills against the armholes of the front and back panel. See that the back edge of the frill is against the back panel and the front edge against the front panel.
10 Stitch bias binding around the armhole. The sides of the frills are stitched at the same time.
11 Gather the neckline until it is 12″ (31cm), 13″ (33cm) or 14″ (35cm) wide, according to size.
12 Stitch bias binding around the neckline.
13 Turn in and stitch the hemline of the dress.

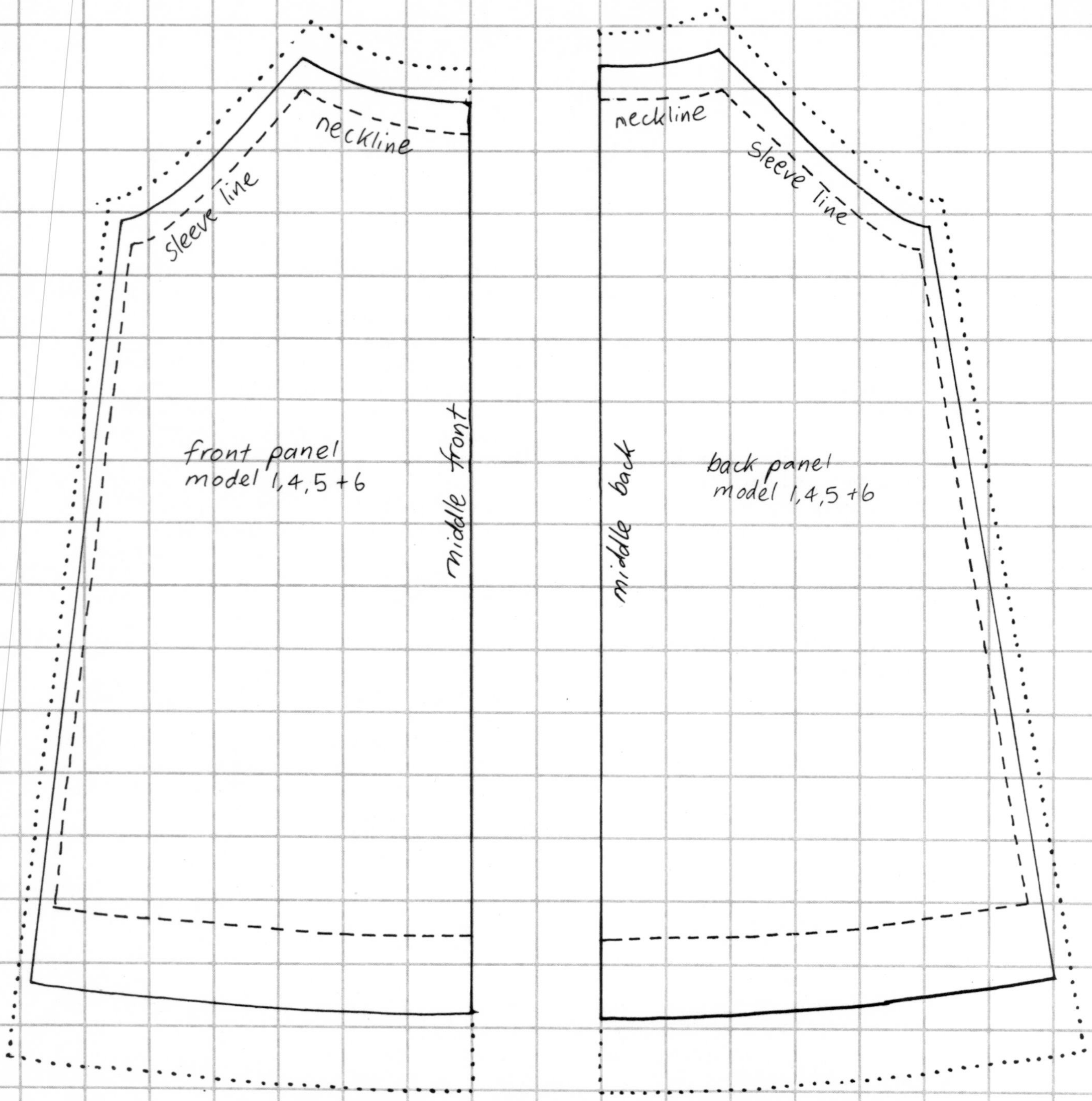

neckline

sleeve line

front panel
model 1, 4, 5 + 6

middle front

neckline

sleeve line

back panel
model 1, 4, 5 + 6

middle back

142

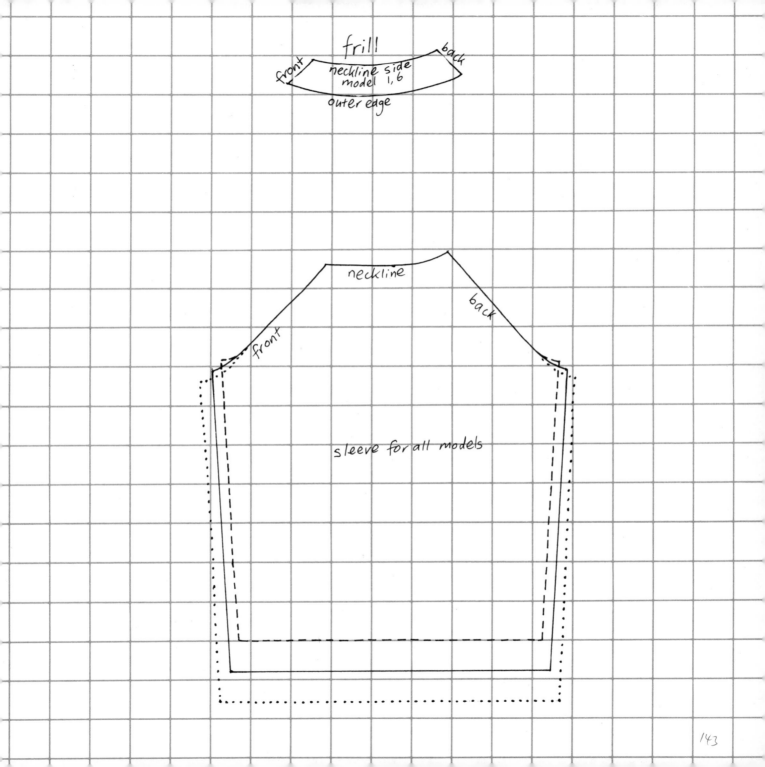

frill

front

back

neckline side
model 1, 6

outer edge

neckline

front

back

sleeve for all models

143

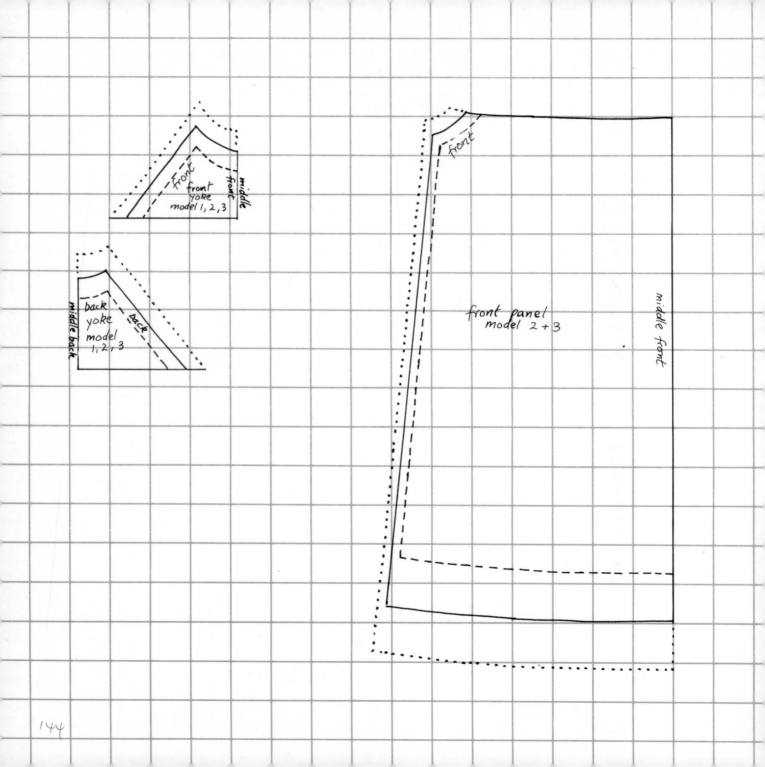

front
front
yoke
model 1, 2, 3
middle front

back
yoke
model 1, 2, 3
back
middle back

front
front panel
model 2 + 3
middle front

144

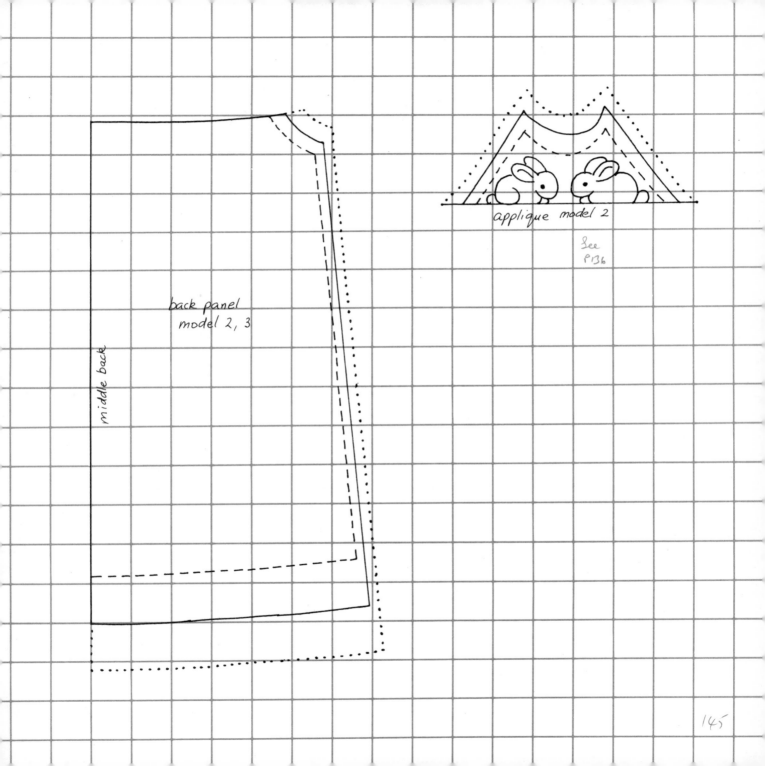

back panel
model 2, 3

middle back

applique model 2

See
P136

145

1

2

3

4

Pants, sunsuit, overalls

Size by age: *3 years,   5 years,   7 years*
Height of child: *38" (98cm), 43" (110cm), 47" (122cm)*
Fabrics: *Sturdy fabrics such as: twill, denim, corduroy, ticking, velveteen, needle-cord, velvet.*
The overalls can be made out of thinner fabric such as: poplin, flannel.

PANTS   Model 1

Pattern pieces: pants front, pants back
Fabric needed: 36" (90cm) wide: 2½yd (2.15m)
                 54" (140cm) wide: 1⅜yd (1.20m)
Notions: 26" (65cm) elastic for each casing
                 optional: ribbon or tape for side seams

Sewing instructions:
1. Reproduce the pattern pieces on 2 x 2" (5 x 5cm) dressmaker's pattern paper. Mark the position of the casings and plan for seam allowance.
2. With right sides together fold the fabric in half and pin the pieces to it.
3. Cut out 1½" (4cm) extra along the top edge of the pants. At the end of the legs allow an extra 1" (2.5cm) for seam allowance. If making pants with elastic in the ends of the legs, cut 2¾" (7cm) extra around the hemlines. The remaining edges have an extra ⅜-¾" (1-2cm) for seam allowance.
4. Zigzag around the edges of the pieces.
5. Stitch the inside leg seams of the front and the back together. Press the seams open.
6. Stitch the crotch seams together. Leave the top edge (the part which is to be folded over) of the middle back open.
7. Stitch the side seams together. At the same time stitch a length of ribbon or tape into the seam, having part of this ribbon showing on the right side at the top of the seam. You can also stitch the side seams first (without adding ribbon or tape) and then stitch a decorative band on top of the seam.
8. Turn in 1" (2.5cm) along the hemlines of the legs and stitch them ⅝" (1.5cm) from the edge. If the hemlines are to be elasticated, leave a small opening and insert the elastic into it. Stitch the ends of the elastic together and then stitch up the opening.
9. Turn in 3" (8cm) along the top edge of the pants. Stitch the casings all the way around. Insert the elastic and stitch the ends together. Stitch up the openings.

SUNSUIT   Model 2

Pattern pieces: front panel, back panel, shoulder straps, front facing, back facing
Fabric needed: 36" (90cm) wide: 2¼yd (2.0m)
                 54" (140cm) wide: 1⅛yd (1.05m)
Notions: 2 fasteners for the shoulder straps,
                 1½yd (1.30m) cord

Sewing instructions:
1. Reproduce the pattern pieces on 2 x 2" (5 x 5cm) dressmaker's pattern paper. Remember to plan for seam allowance.
2. With right sides together fold the fabric in half and pin the pieces to it, having the middle front and middle back of the facing against the fabric fold.
3. Cut out the pieces with an extra ⅜-¾" (1-2cm) for seam allowance.
4. Zigzag around the edges of the pieces.

5 Stitch the inside leg seams of the front and back together. Press them open.

6 Stitch the middle front and the middle back together all the way around. Clip the curve in the seam allowance and press the seam to one side. Stitch once again close to the seam.

7 Fold the shoulder straps in half and stitch along the edges. Turn them and pin them with the diagonal edge to the back panel.

8 With right sides together, stitch the front facing along the upper edge and the armholes to the front panel. Clip the curve in the seam allowance.

9 Stitch the back facing along the upper edge and armholes, at the same time stitching the shoulder straps. Clip the curve in the seam allowance.

10 Stitch the side seams together, also the side seams of the front and back facing. Press the seams open.

11 Turn the garment right side out, having the facing on the inside. Top-stitch around the upper edge.

12 Sew the sides of the facing to the side seams at the bottom edge.

13 Fold in the hemline of the legs and stitch them ¾" (2cm) from the bottom edge.

14 Attach fasteners to the shoulder straps and tie the cord around the waist.

OVERALLS WITH FRONT POCKET *Model 3*

Pattern pieces: front panel, back panel, shoulder strap, pocket, front facing, back facing
Fabric needed: 36" (90cm) wide: 3¼yd (3.0m)
54" (140cm) wide: 1¾yd (1.55m)
Notions: 2 metal fasteners,
14" (35cm) ruched lingerie elastic 1⅛" (3cm) wide, 2 buttons, zipper

Sewing instructions:
Follow the instructions for model 2. The only variations are in steps 1, 2, 3 and 6. Step 10a is added.

1 Reproduce the pattern pieces on 2 x 2" (5 x 5cm) dressmaker's pattern paper. Remember to plan for seam allowance. Mark the position of the pocket and where the elastic is to be stitched on.

2 With right sides together, fold the fabric in half and pin the pieces to it, having the middle of the back facing against the fabric fold.

3 Cut out the middle front of the front panel and the front facing with an extra ¾" (2cm) for seam allowance. The remaining edges with an extra ⅜-¾" (1-2cm) for seam allowance.

6 Stitch the middle back seam and the lowest part of the middle front together all the way around. Clip the curve in the seam allowance and press the seam open. Stitch the zipper into the middle front seam. (See p14 for how to insert zipper.)

10a Stitch the ruched lingerie elastic where indicated on the pattern. The ends of the elastic are stitched in with the pockets. Turn in and stitch the seam allowance of the pockets. Stitch along the top edge of the pockets. Stitch the pockets on to the front panel. If desired, stitch on a loop made of bias binding at the same time. To make the loop, cut a length of bias binding, fold it in half lengthwise and stitch around the edges.

OVERALLS WITH SIDE POCKETS *Model 4*

Pattern pieces: front panel, back panel, shoulder strap, front facing, back facing, front pocket, side pocket
Fabric needed: 36" (90cm) wide: 3¼yd (3.0m)
54" (140cm) wide: 1¾yd (1.55m)
Notions: 2 metal fasteners, 2 buttons

Sewing instructions:

Follow the instructions for model 2. The only variations are in steps 1, 6 and 10. Step 15 is added.

1 Reproduce the pattern pieces on 2 x 2″ (5 x 5cm) dressmaker's pattern paper. Remember to plan for seam allowance. Mark the position of the pockets.

6 Turn in and press three of the seam allowances on the front pocket – the upper edge, the lower edge and the side that is not stitched in with the middle front seam. Stitch along the upper edge. Stitch the side which has been turned in and the lower edge on to the front panel. Now stitch the middle front and middle back together all the way around, stitching the pocket at the same time. Clip the curve in the seam alowance, press the seam allo-wance to one side and stitch once again parallel to the seam.

10 Stitch the side seams together. On one side leave 4½″ (12cm) open at the top. Also leave the facing open on the same side. Press the seams open. Turn in the facing. Fold in the seam allowance of the facing and the opening. Stitch along the edges of the opening. At the same time, stitch on to the front of the opening 2 loops made of bias binding. Whilst doing this, the side of the facing at the top of the opening is also stitched down. This means that the loops are stitched between the front facing and the front panel. To make the loops, measure the amount of bias binding needed for each button. Cut a length for two and fold it in half. Stitch around the edges, cut in half and form each piece into a loop. Sew on the buttons opposite the loops.

15 Press in the seam allowance of the side pockets all the way around. Stitch along the upper edge.

Stitch the pockets where indicated on the pattern. If you wish, stitch a loop made of bias binding to the bottom of the pocket at the same time.

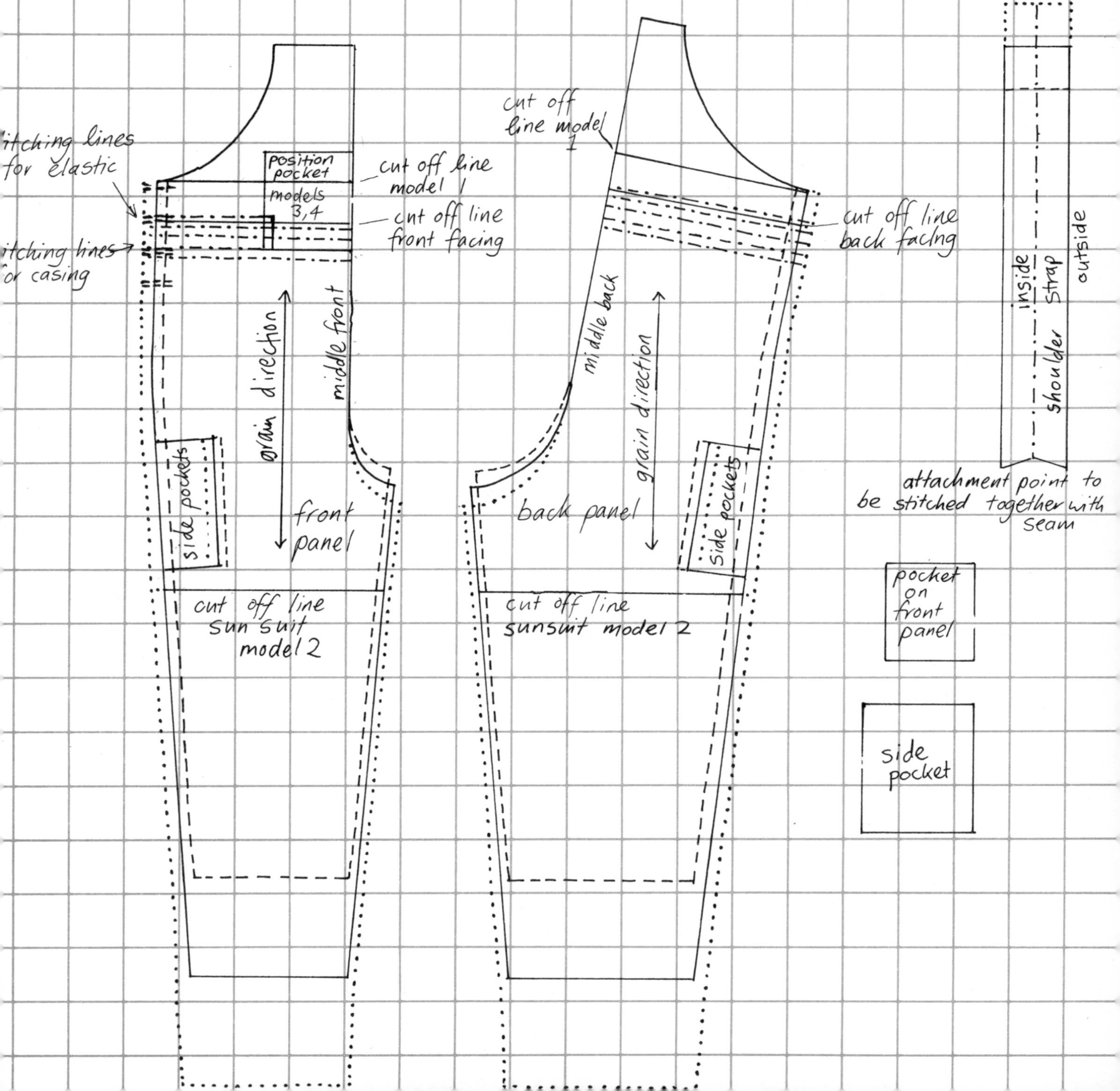

stitching lines
for elastic

stitching lines
for casing

position
pocket
models
3,4

cut off line
model 1

cut off line
front facing

cut off line
sun suit
model 2

grain direction

middle front

front
panel

side pockets

cut off
line model
1

cut off line
back facing

middle back

grain direction

back panel

side pockets

cut off line
sunsuit model 2

inside

shoulder strap

outside

attachment point to
be stitched together with
seam

pocket
on
front
panel

side
pocket

4 5 6

Tops and T-shirts for older children

Size by age: 3 years, 5 years, 7 years
Height of child: 38" (98cm), 43" (110cm), 47" (122cm)
Fabrics: *Stretch fabrics such as: jersey, terry-cloth, tricot or soft fabrics such as flannel(ette), poplin, crepe, viyella.*

Stretch fabrics should always be stitched with a narrow zigzag stitch. This gives the seam some elasticity.

LONG TOP WITH ELASTICATED WAISTLINE

Model 1

Pattern pieces: front panel, back panel, casing
Fabric needed: 54" (140cm) wide: 1⅜yd (1.25m)
Notions: 2⅞yd (2.70m) bias binding, 4 buttons, 1⅜yd (1.20m) elastic ⅜" (1cm) wide or ¾yd (70cm) bias binding 2¼yd (2.0m) cord, 4 buttons, 1⅜yd (1.20m) elastic ⅜" (1cm) wide

Sewing instructions:

1 Reproduce the pattern pieces on 2 x 2" (5 x 5cm) dressmaker's pattern paper. Remember to plan for seam allowance. Mark the position of the casing on the front and back panels.
2 With right sides together fold the fabric in half and pin the pieces to it, having the middle front, middle back and casing against the fabric fold.
3 Cut out the neckline without a seam allowance. The bottom edge of the top and the sleeves need an extra 1" (2.5cm) for seam allowance. The remaining edges need an extra ⅜-¾" (1-2cm) for seam allowance.
4 Zigzag around the edges of the pieces.

5 Stitch the underarm side seams together. Leave an opening where the casing is to be. Clip the curve in the seam allowance and press the seams open.
6 Stitch the shoulder seams together. Leave an opening of 2½" (6cm) next to the neckline on both sides. Press the seams open. Stitch along the edges of the opening. At the same time, stitch a loop made of bias binding on to the front side of both neckline openings. To make the loops, measure the amount of binding needed for each button. Cut a length long enough for two loops. Fold it in half lengthwise and stitch around the edges. Cut in half and form each length into a loop.
7 Finish the neckline with bias binding. For the front neckline allow 5" (12cm) more bias binding than the width of the neckline. Leave 2¼" (6cm) loose on both sides, and form into loops.
8 Turn in and press the seam allowance around the casings. Stitch the casings where indicated to the insides of the front and back panels. Thread two lengths of bias binding through the casings or two cords each measuring 1⅜yd (1.0m) in length. If using bais binding, fold it in half lengthwise and stitch around the edges.
9 Fold in the hemline of the garment and stitch ⅝" (1.5cm) from the edge. Leave a small opening. Insert the elastic and stitch the two ends together. Stitch up the opening.
10 Turn in the bottom ends of the sleeves and stitch ⅝" (1.5cm) from the edge. Leave a small opening. Insert the elastic and stitch the ends together. Stitch up the opening.
11 Sew buttons to the neckline opening, opposite the loops.

TOP WITH DIAGONAL ROW OF BUTTONS *Model 2*

Pattern pieces: front panel, back panel, sleeve
Fabric needed: 54" (140cm) wide: 1¼yd (1.15m)
Notions: 1½yd (1.30m) bias binding, 5 buttons, 1⅜yd (1.20m) elastic

Sewing instructions:

1 Reproduce the pattern pieces on 2 x 2" (5 x 5cm) dressmaker's pattern paper. Remember to plan for seam allowance. Cut off the sleeve where indicated on the front and back panels and join the upper arm seam edges together so the sleeve is cut out as one piece. Mark the position of the loops and buttons. Mark the farthest point reached by the wrapover section.
2 With right sides together fold the fabric in half and pin the pieces to it.
3 Cut out the neckline and the top edge of the wrapover without a seam allowance. The bottom edge of the sleeves and the bottom edge of the garment need an extra 1" (2.5cm) for seam allowance. The remaining edges need an extra ⅜-¾" (1-2cm) for seam allowance.
4 Zigzag around the edges of the pieces.
5 Stitch the shoulder seams. Press the seam open.
6 Finish the neckline and the upper edge of the wrapover with bias binding. Stitch five bias binding loops where indicated at the same time. To make the loops, measure the amount of binding needed for each button. Cut a length to make five loops, fold in half lengthwise and stitch around the edges. Cut into 5 pieces and form into loops. Fold the wrapover from the back panel over the front panel until it reaches the marked position. Pin in place.
7 Stitch the sleeves to the panels. On one side the sides of the wrapovers are stitched at the same time. Press the seams open.
8 Stitch the underarm side seams. Clip the curve in the seam allowance and press the seams open.
9 Turn in the bottom edge of the sleeves and stitch ⅝" (1.5cm) from the edge. Leave a small opening. Insert the elastic and stitch the ends together. Stitch up the opening.
10 Turn in the hemline and stitch along ⅝" (1.5cm) from the bottom edge. Leave a small opening. Insert the elastic into this and stitch both ends of elastic together. Stitch up the opening.
11 Sew buttons where indicated opposite the loops.

SHORT-SLEEVED T-SHIRT *Model 4*

Pattern pieces: front panel, back panel
Fabric needed: 36" (90cm) wide: 1½yd (1.20m)
54" (140cm) wide: ¾yd (0.60m)
Notions: 30" (75cm) bias binding, 4 buttons, 30" (75cm) elastic ⅜"(1cm) wide. Optional: a strip of fabric measuring 10" (24cm) long, 36" (90cm) wide and 1½yd (1.20m) of decorative ribbon or tape

Sewing instructions:

1 Reproduce the pattern pieces on 2 x 2" (5 x 5cm) dressmaker's pattern paper and remember to plan for seam allowance. If you wish to insert a strip of contrasting fabric into the front and back panel, mark this on the pattern. Cut out the pieces.
2 With right sides together fold the fabric in half and pin the pieces to it, having the middle front and middle back against the fabric fold.

3 Cut out the neckline without a seam allowance. The hemline with an extra 1″ (2.5cm) for seam allowance. The remaining edges with an extra ⅜-¾″ (1-2cm). If you are going to insert a contrasting strip in the front and back panels, as shown on the drawing, cut out the band from a different fabric.

4 Zigzag around the edges of the pieces.

5 Stitch the different sections of the front and back panels together. Stitch matching tape or ribbon above the band.
This step only applies if you have cut the panels into different sections.

6 Stitch the side seams together. Clip the curve in the seam allowance and press the seams open.

7 Stitch the shoulder seams together. Leave an opening of 2¼″ (6cm) at the neckline on both sides. Press the seams open. Turn in and stitch the edges of the openings. At the same time, stitch on a loop made of bias binding half way along the front of each opening. To make loops, measure the amount of binding needed for each button. Cut enough binding for two, fold it in half and stitch around the edges. Cut in half and form into loops.

8 Finish the neckline with bias binding. For the front neckline allow 5″ (12cm) more than you need for the neckline. Leave 2½″ (6cm) tape loose on each side and make into loops. Stitch on buttons opposite loops.

9 Turn in the hemline of the T-shirt and stitch ⅝″ (1.5cm) from the edge. Leave a small opening. Insert the elastic and stitch the ends together. Stitch up the opening.

10 Turn in the ends of the sleeves and stitch ⅜″ (1cm) from the edge.

LONG-SLEEVED TOP WITH KNITTED CUFFS
Model 3

Pattern pieces: front panel, back panel
Fabric needed: 54″ (140cm) wide: 1⅜yd (1.20m)
Notions: 4″ (12cm) zipper, ½yd (45cm) bias binding, knitted cuffs for the sleeves and the bottom edge of the garment

Sewing instructions:

1 Reproduce the pattern pieces on 2 x 2″ (5 x 5cm) dressmaker's pattern paper. Remember to plan for seam allowance.

2 With right sides together, fold the fabric in half and pin the pieces to it, having the middle front and middle back against the fabric fold.

3 Cut out the neckline without a seam allowance. The remaining edges with an extra ⅜-¾″ (1-2cm) for seam allowance.

4 Zigzag around the edges of the pieces.

5 Stitch the underarm side seams. Clip the curve in the seam allowance and press the seams open.

6 Stitch the upper arm seams together. Leave an opening of 4″ (12cm) for the zipper on one side at the neckline. Press the seams open and stitch the zipper into the seam. (See p14 for how to insert a zipper.)

7 Finish the neckline with bias binding.

8 Stitch knitted cuffs on to the ends of the sleeves.

9 Stitch the knitted cuff on to the hemline.

T-SHIRT WITH ENVELOPE NECK
Model 5

Pattern pieces: front panel, back panel
Fabric needed: 36″ (90cm) wide: 1⅜yd (1.20m)
54″ (140cm) wide: ¾yd (0.60m)

Notions: 3¾yd (3.50m) bias binding, 2 buttons, 24″ (60cm) ruched lingerie elastic 1″ (2.5cm) wide

Sewing instructions:

1 Reproduce the pattern pieces on 2 x 2″ (5 x 5cm) dressmaker's pattern paper. Remember to plan for seam allowance. Mark the position of the loops and buttons and the point reached by the neckline flap.
2 With right sides together, fold the fabric in half and pin the pieces to it, having the middle front and middle back against the fabric fold.
3 Cut out the top edge of the front and back panel, the bottom edge of the sleeves and the bottom edge of the T-shirt without a seam allowance. The remaining edges with an extra ⅜-¾″ (1-2cm).
4 Zigzag around the edges of the pieces.
5 Stitch bias binding along the top edge of the back panel. At the same time, stitch on loops made of bias binding. To make loops, measure amount of binding needed for each button. Cut a length for two loops, fold in half lengthwise and stitch around the edges. Cut in half and form into loops.
6 Stitch bias binding along the top edge of the front panel.
7 Fold the flap on the back panel over the front panel until it reaches the point marked on the pattern.
8 Finish the side of the flaps with bias binding. In so doing, the flaps of the front panel and back panel are stitched together on the side edge.
9 Stitch the side seams. Clip the curve in the seam allowance and press the seams open.
10 Stitch bias binding around the hemline.
11 Stitch ruched lingerie elastic where indicated.
12 Sew buttons on opposite the loops.

MINI TOP WITH SHOULDER TIES

Pattern pieces: front panel, back panel
Fabric needed: 36″ (90cm) wide: ⅞yd (0.80m)
54″ (140cm) wide: ½yd (0.40m)
Notions: 1⅛yd (1.0m) bias binding

Sewing instructions:

1 Reproduce the pattern pieces on 2 x 2″ (5 x 5cm) dressmaker's pattern paper. Remember to plan for seam allowance.
2 With right sides together, fold the fabric in half and pin the pieces to it, having the middle front and middle back against the fabric fold.
3 Cut out the neckline without a seam allowance. The remaining edges with an extra ⅜-¾″ (1-2cm) for seam allowance.
4 Zigzag around the edges of the pieces.
5 Stitch the side seams together. Clip the curve in the seam allowance and press the seams open.
6 Stitch the shoulder seams together. Leave an opening of 2½″ (6cm) at the neckline on both sides. Press the seams open and turn in and stitch the sides of the opening.
7 Finish the neckline with bias binding. For both the front neckline and the back neckline allow 24″ (60cm) more bias binding than needed. Leave 12″ (30cm) of tape loose on both sides.
8 Turn in the hemline and stitch.
9 Turn in the ends of the sleeves and stitch.

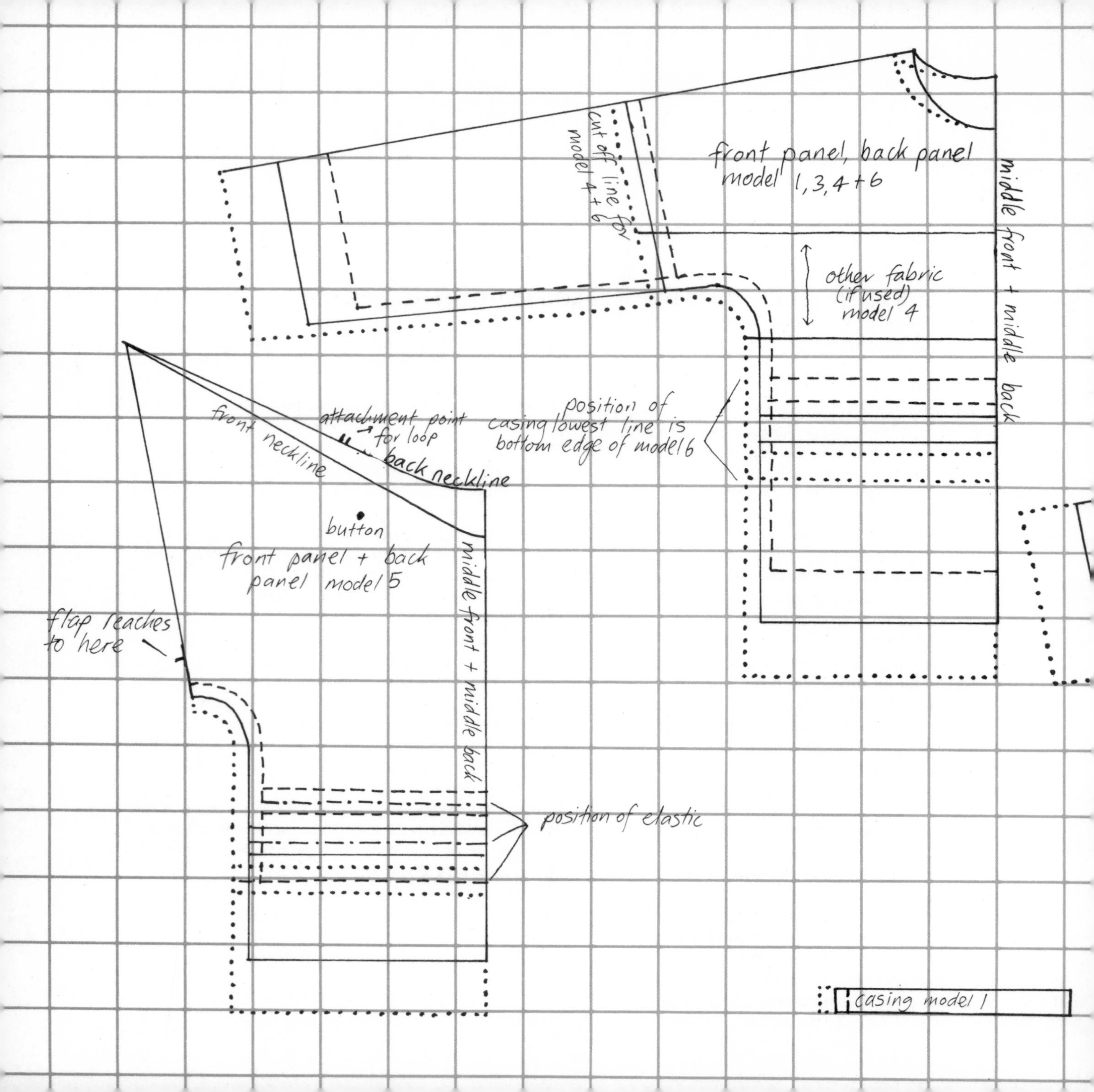

cut off line for model 4 + 6

front panel, back panel
model 1, 3, 4 + 6

middle front + middle back

other fabric (if used) model 4

front neckline

attachment point for loop

back neckline

position of casing lowest line is bottom edge of model 6

button

front panel + back panel model 5

middle front + middle back

flap reaches to here

position of elastic

casing model 1

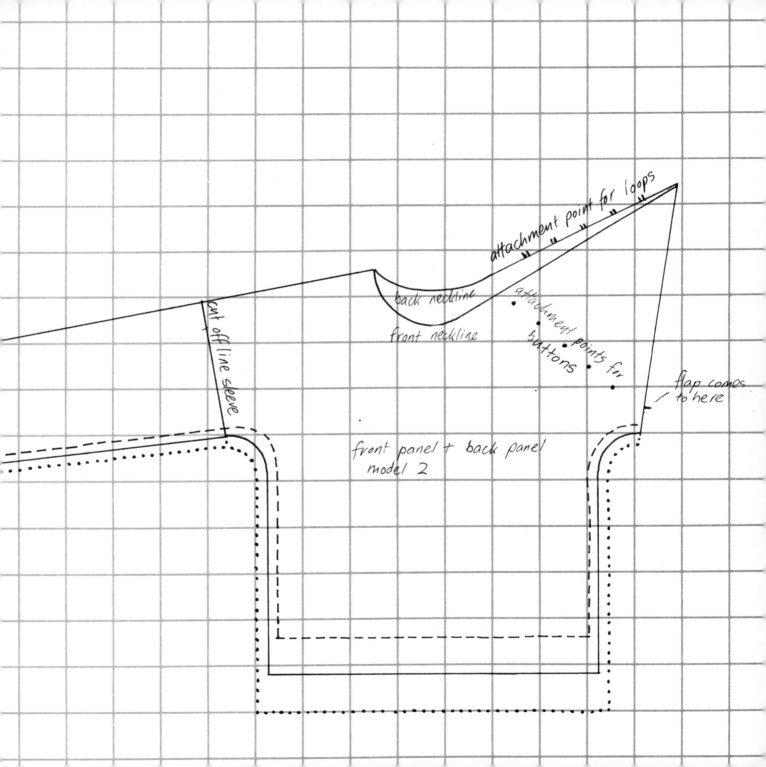

attachment point for loops

back neckline

front neckline

attachment points for buttons

flap comes to here

cut off line sleeve

front panel + back panel
model 2

Jackets, coats, wrapover dress and blouse, skirt, pants

Size by age: *2 years, 4 years, 6 years*
Height of child: *36" (92cm), 40" (104cm), 45" (116cm)*
Fabrics: *You can use all kinds of fabrics for these garments. Soft and strong cottons such as: poplin, flannelette, gabardine, corduroy, needlecord, velveteen, twill.*
Woollen fabrics such as: jersey, bouclé.
Linings: flannelette, acrylic fur, flannel.

WRAPOVER DRESS   Model 1

Pattern pieces: front panel, back panel
Fabric needed: 54" (140cm) wide: 1½yd (1.40m)
Notions: 6yd (5.50m) bias binding

Sewing instructions:

1 Reproduce the pattern pieces on 2 x 2" (5 x 5cm) dressmaker's pattern paper. Remember to plan for seam allowance. Mark the side seam where the opening for the tie belt is to be.
2 With right sides together fold the fabric in half and pin the pieces to it, having the middle back against the fabric fold.
3 Cut out the top edge of the wrapover, the neckline, the side edge of the wrapover, the hemline and the armholes without a seam allowance. The remaining edges with an extra ⅜-¾" (1-2cm) for seam allowance.
4 Zigzag around the edges of the pieces.
5 Stitch the shoulder seams, press the seams open.
6 Stitch bias binding around the armholes.
7 Stitch the side seams together. Leave an opening at the waistline, as indicated on the pattern, to insert the tie belt. Clip the curve in the seam allow-ance and press the seams open.
8 Stitch bias binding around the hemline and the sides of the wrapover.
9 Stitch bias binding around the neckline and the top edge of the wrapover. Leave 28" (70cm) loose on each side for the tie fastening.

SLEEVELESS PULLOVER   Model 2

Pattern pieces: front panel, back panel, casing, neckline facing
Fabric needed: 36" (90cm) wide: 1¾yd (1.55m)
54" (140cm) wide: ⅞yd (0.80m)
Notions: 4yd (4.0m) cord, 8" (20cm) zipper

Sewing instructions:

1 Reproduce the pattern pieces on 2 x 2" (5 x 5cm) dressmaker's pattern paper. Remember to plan for seam allowance. Mark the position of the casings on the front and back panel. Join the front and back facing shoulder seams together to make one piece.
2 With right sides together fold the fabric in half and pin the pieces to it, having the middle front of the front panel and middle front of the neckline facing against the fabric fold.
3 Cut out an extra 1" (2.5cm) for seam allowance on the hemline. The remaining edges with an extra ⅜-¾" (1-2cm) for seam allowance.
4 Zigzag around the edges of the pieces.
5 Stitch the side seams together. Leave ¾" (2cm) open at the waistline and 1½" (4cm) at the bottom edge. Clip the curve in the seam allowance and press the seams open.

6 Stitch the shoulder seams together. Press the seams open.
7 Stitch the neckline facing to the neckline. Clip the curve in the seam allowance and cut off the corner at the middle front diagonally.
8 Stitch the middle back seam, stopping 8″ (20cm) from the neckline. Press the seam open.
9 Stitch the zipper into the opening. (See p14 for how to insert zipper.)
10 Turn in the neckline facing. Turn in the seam allowance next to the middle back seam and stitch all the way around the neckline.
11 Turn in the seam allowance around the edges of the casings. Stitch the casings on to the inside of the front and back panels as indicated.
12 Turn in the ends of the sleeves and stitch ⅜″ (1cm) from the edge.
13 Turn in the hemline and stitch ⅝″ (1.5cm) from the bottom edge. Leave the sides open. Thread a cord measuring 1yd (1.0m) through each casing.

PANTS

Pattern pieces: pants front, pants back, band for the ends of the legs
Fabric needed: 36″ (90cm) wide: 1½yd (1.35m)
  54″ (140cm) wide: 1yd (0.90m)
Notions: 26″ (65cm) elastic ⅜″ (1cm) wide

Sewing instructions:
Follow the instructions for model 1 on page 41 The ends of the legs are gathered to match the width of the bands. Stitch the side seams of the band together. Press the seams open. Turn in and iron the seam allowance on both sides and fold and press the bands in half. Stitch them around the gathered ends of the legs.

COAT

Pattern pieces: top section front panel, bottom section front panel, top section back panel, bottom section back panel, pocket
Fabric needed: 54″ (140cm) wide: 1⅞yd (1.65m)
Lining: 54″ (140cm) wide: 1⅞yd (1.65m)
Notions: snap fasteners

Sewing instructions:
1 Reproduce the pattern pieces on 2 x 2″ (5 x 5cm) dressmaker's pattern paper. Remember to plan for seam allowance. Mark the position of the pockets.
2 With right sides together fold the fabric in half and pin the pieces to it. The bottom section of the front panel, the top section of the back panel and the bottom section of the back panel are placed against the fold.
3 Cut out the pieces with an extra ⅜-¾″ (1-2cm) for seam allowance.
4 Repeat steps 2 and 3 with the lining fabric.
5 Zigzag around the edges of the pieces.
6 Stitch the shoulder seams and press them open.
7 Stitch the underarm seams. Clip the curve in the seam allowance and press the seams open.
8 Stitch the shoulder seams of the lining fabric and press them open.
9 Stitch the underarm seams of the lining fabric. Clip the curve in the seam allowance and press the seams open.
10 With the right sides together, fit the top section and the facing made of lining fabric into each other.
11 Stitch the bottom edges of the sleeves together.
12 Stitch the neckline and the flap together. Clip the curve in the seam allowance and cut off the corners diagonally. Turn the top section right side out.

13 Top-stitch around the edges of the sleeves. Topstitch along the edge of the neckline and flap.

14 Stitch the side seams of the bottom section and press the seams open.

15 Press in the seam allowance of the pockets all the way around. Stitch along the top edge. Stitch the pockets on as indicated on the pattern.

16 Stitch the top section to the bottom section. Take care that the flap is on the right side. Press the seam down.

17 Stitch the side seams of the bottom section of the lining and press the seams open.

18 Turn in and press the seam allowance of the bottom section of the lining along the top edge. Pin both bottom sections together along the top edge. Stitch on the right side of the coat, keeping close to the seam. In doing so, the bottom section of the lining is stitched on at the same time.

19 Turn in both hemlines until they are level with the bottom edge of the pockets and stitch together all the way around.

20 Attach the snap fasteners where indicated.

COAT WITH TIE FASTENING   Model 4

Pattern pieces: top section front panel, bottom section front panel, back panel
Fabric needed: 54" (140cm) wide: 1⅞yd (1.65m)
Notions: 2⅞yd (2.60m) bias binding

Sewing instructions:

1 Reproduce the pattern pieces on 2 x 2" (5 x 5cm) dressmaker's pattern paper. Remember to plan for seam allowance. Mark the position of the pockets and the place where a tie is stitched into the upper arm seam.

2 With right sides together fold the fabric in half and pin the pieces to it, having the middle back and middle front of the bottom section against the fold.

3 Cut out the neckline, the upper edge and the side of the flap, and the bottom edge of the back panel without a seam allowance. The remaining edges with an extra ⅜-¾" (1-2cm) for seam allowance.

4 Zigzag around the edges of the pieces.

5 Stitch the shoulder seams. At the same time, stitch on a 12" (34cm) length of bias binding on each side where indicated on the pattern. First, fold the binding in half lengthwise and stitch around the edges. Depending on which flap is to be on top, on one side the binding hangs out on the outside and on the other side it hangs out on the inside.

6 Stitch bias binding around the neckline and along the top of the flap.

7 Stitch bias binding along the sides of the flap. Allow 12" (30cm) more bias binding than you need for the side and leave 12" (30cm) loose at the top.

8 Stitch the top section of the front panel to the bottom section of the front panel. See that the flap is on the right side. Press the seam down and top-stich close to the seam.

9 Stitch the underarm side seams. Clip the curve in the seam allowance and press them open.

10 Gather the bottom edges of the sleeves until they are 8" (20cm) wide. Stitch bias binding around them.

11 Turn in and press the seam allowance of the pockets, except for the bottom edge. Stitch along the top edge and stitch the pockets on where indicated on the pattern. The bottom edge of the pocket must be level with the hemline of the coat.

12 Finish the hemline of the coat with bias binding. At the same time the bottom edges of the pockets are stitched on.

WRAPOVER BLOUSE   Model 5

Pattern pieces: front panel, back panel
Fabric needed: 36″ (90cm) wide: 1⅛yd (1.0m)
               54″ (140cm) wide: 1⅛yd (1.0m)
Notions: 3yd (2.80m) bias binding,
               30″ (75cm) ruched lingerie elastic ¾″ (2cm) wide

Sewing instructions:
 1 Reproduce the pattern pieces on 2 x 2″ (5 x 5cm) dressmaker's pattern paper. Mark the position of the ruched lingerie elastic and plan for seam allowance.
 2 With right sides together, fold the fabric in half and pin the pieces to it, having the middle back against the fabric fold.
 3 Cut out the neckline, the top edge of the wrapover, the bottom edge of the sleeves and the hemline of the blouse without a seam allowance. The remaining edges with an extra ⅜-¾″ (1-2cm).
 4 Zigzag around the edges of the pieces.
 5 Stitch the shoulder seams and press them open.
 6 Stitch bias binding around the neckline and the top edge of the wrapover.
 7 Stitch bias binding around the bottom edge of the sleeves.
 8 Stitch the side seams, stitching the side of the wrapover at the same time. Be sure that the right wrapover is on top. Clip the curve in the seam allowance and press the seams open.
 9 Stitch on ruched lingerie elastic ¾″ (2cm) wide where indicated on the pattern.
10 Stitch bias binding around the hemline.

SKIRT   165

Pattern pieces: skirt front, skirt back
Fabric needed: 36″ (90cm) wide: 1⅜yd (1.20m)
               54″ (140cm) wide: ¾yd (0.60m)
Notions: 30″ (75cm) elastic ⅜″ (1cm) wide

Sewing instructions:
Follow the instructions for model 3 on page 173

JACKET   Model 6

Pattern pieces: top section front panel, bottom section front panel, top section back panel, bottom section back panel, pocket
Fabric needed: 54″ (140cm) wide: ½yd (0.45m)
Notions: knitted cuffs for the ends of the sleeves, hemline of the jacket and top edge of wrapover

Sewing instructions:
 1 Reproduce the pattern pieces on 2 x 2″ (5 x 5cm) dressmaker's pattern paper. Mark the position of the pocket and plan for seam allowance.
 2 With right sides together fold the fabric in half and pin the pieces to it. The top section of the back panel, the bottom section of the back panel and the bottom section of the front panel are placed against the fabric fold.
 3 Cut out the pieces with an extra ⅜-¾″ (1-2cm) for seam allowance.
 4 Zigzag around the edges of the pieces.
 5 Stitch the shoulder seams and press them open.
 6 Stitch the underarm seams. Clip the curve in the seam allowance and press them open.

7   Stitch the knitted cuff around the neckline and the top edge of the wrapover. Clip the seam allowance of the neckline.

8   Stitch the knitted cuffs on to the sleeves.

9   Turn in and press the seam allowance around the pocket. Stitch along the top edge. Stitch the pocket to the bottom section of the front panel where indicated on the pattern.

10 Stitch the side seams of the bottom section of the front panel and the bottom section of the back panel together. Press the seams open.

11 Stitch the top section and bottom section together. Press the seam down and top-stitch all the way around close to the seam.

12 Stitch the knitted cuff on to the hemline of the jacket.

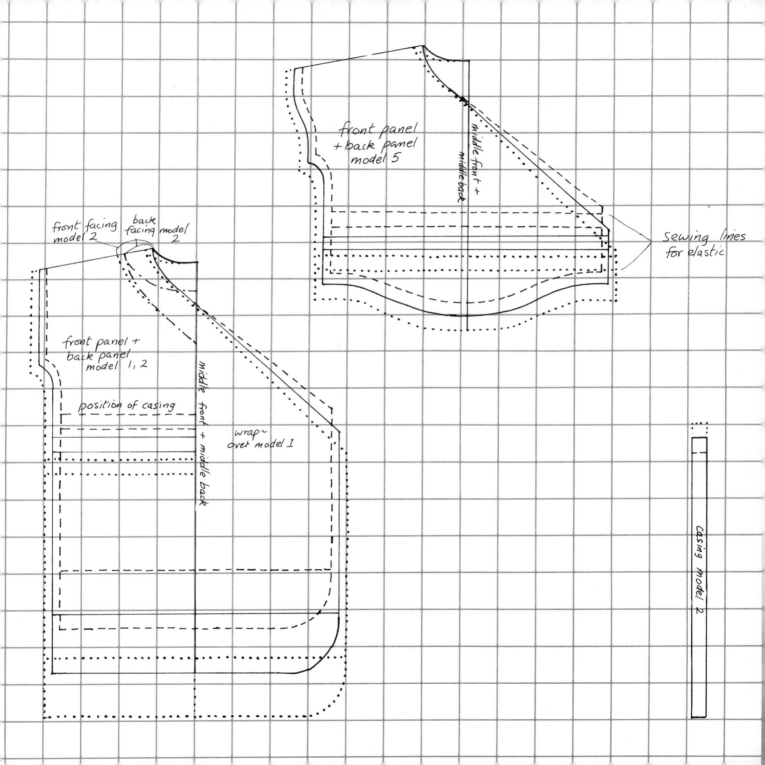

front panel
+ back panel
model 5

middle front +
middle back

sewing lines
for elastic

front facing
model 2

back
facing model
2

front panel +
back panel
model 1, 2

position of casing

middle front + middle back

wrap~
over model 1

casing model 2

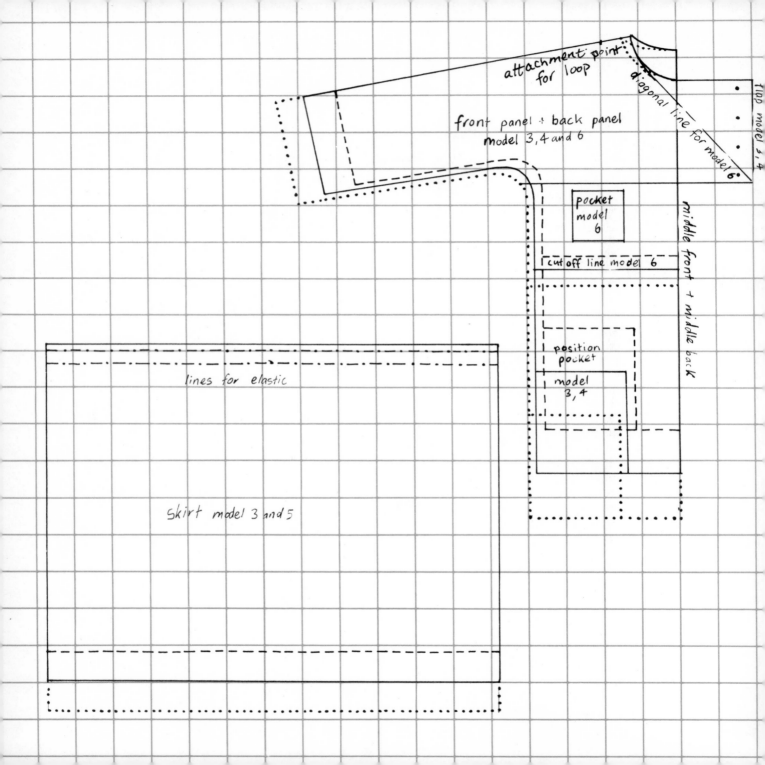

attachment point
for loop

front panel + back panel
model 3,4 and 6

diagonal line for model 6

flap model 3, 4

middle front + middle back

pocket
model
6

cut off line model 6

position
pocket

model
3,4

lines for elastic

Skirt model 3 and 5

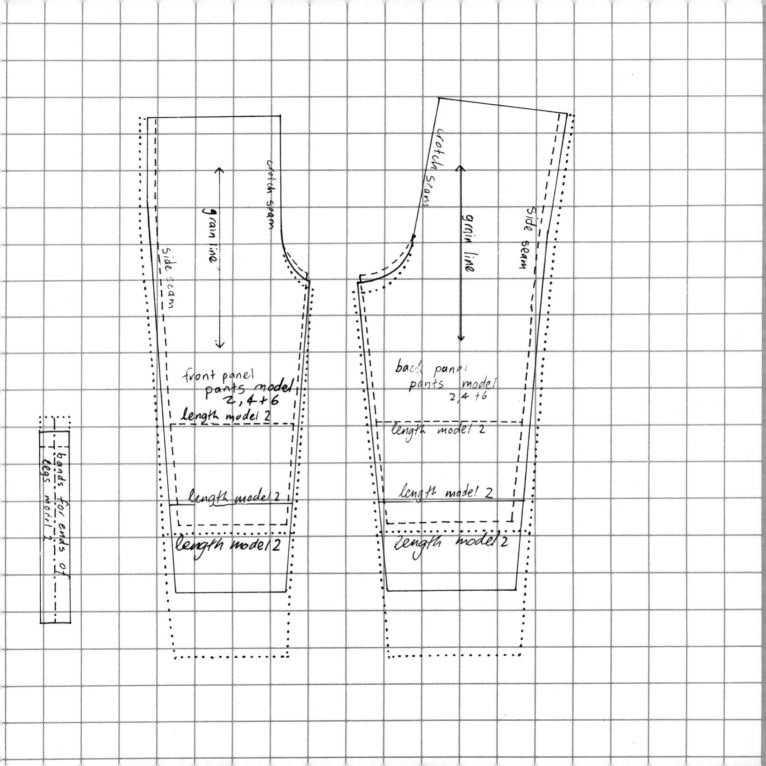

3

4

LIAS

Dress with divided skirt, sundress, skirt, culottes

Size by age: 3 years,   5 years,   7 years
Height of child: 38" (98cm), 43" (110cm), 47" (122cm)
Fabrics: *Soft fabrics such as: poplin, damask, embroidered cotton, crepe batiste, viyella.*

DRESS WITH DIVIDED SKIRT   *Model 1*

Pattern pieces: front panel, back panel
Fabric needed: 36" (90cm) wide: 2¼yd (2.0m)
                     54" (140cm) wide: 2¼yd (2.0m)
Notions: elastic: 26" (65cm) for each casing

Sewing instructions:

1 Reproduce the pattern pieces on 2 x 2" (5 x 5cm) dressmaker's pattern paper. Remember to plan for seam allowance.
2 With right sides together fold the fabric in half and pin the pieces to it.
3 For the upper edge of size 38" (98cm), cut 6" (15cm) extra, for size 43" (110cm), 6½" (17cm) extra and for size 47" (122cm), 7½" (19cm) extra. The remaining edges with an extra ⅜-¾" (1-2cm) for seam allowance.
4 Zigzag around the edges of the pieces.
5 Stitch the inside leg seams together. Press them open.
6 Stitch the middle front and middle back together all the way around. Clip the curve in the seam allowance and press the seam open.
7 Stitch the side seams together. Leave the extra section that was cut out along the top open on one side. Press the seams open.
8 Fold in the extra section on the upper edge and stitch the casings all the way around. Start by stitching around the waistline and work your way up.

9 Thread the elastic through the casings and stitch the ends of elastic together.
10 Turn in the hemline and stitch it down.
11 Stitch ties to the front and back panels. On the front panel leave a space of 5½" (14cm) between the tapes, on the back panel leave a space of 1½" (4cm). To make the ties, cut out strips of fabric measuring 18" (45cm) long and 1½" (4cm) wide. Turn in and press ⅜" (1cm) around the edges, fold them in half and stitch around the edges.

SUNDRESS   *Model 2*

Pattern pieces: front panel, back panel
Fabric needed: 36" (90cm) wide: 2¼yd (2.0m)
                     54" (140cm) wide: 1¼yd (1.05m)
Notions: elastic: 26" (65cm) for each casing

Sewing instructions:

1 Reproduce the pattern pieces on 2 x 2" (5 x 5cm) dressmaker's pattern paper. Remember to plan for seam allowance.
2 With right sides together fold the fabric in half and pin the pieces to it. Depending on the width of the fabric, place one side against the fabric fold or the middle front and middle back against the fold.
3 For size 38" (98cm), cut out 3" (8cm) extra along the upper edge, for size 43" (110cm), 4" (10cm) extra and for size 47" (122cm), 4¾" (12cm) extra. The remaining edges with an extra ⅜-¾" (1-2cm) for seam allowance.
4 Zigzag around the edges of the pieces.
5 Stitch the side seams. Leave the extra section of fabric that was cut along the upper edge open on one side. Press the seams open.

6 Fold in the extra fabric on the upper edge and stitch casings all the way around.
7 Thread elastic through the casings and stitch the ends of elastic together. Stitch up the openings.
8 Turn in the hemline and stitch it at the desired length.
9 Cut out four strips of fabric 18″ (45cm) long and 1½″ (4cm) wide. Press ⅜″ (1cm) in around the edges, fold them in half and stitch around the edges.
10 Stitch the tapes to the upper edge. On the front panel attach them 3″ (7cm) from the middle front and on the back panel 1¼″ (3cm) from the middle back.

SKIRT   Model 3

Pattern pieces: front panel, back panel
Fabric needed: 36″ (90cm) wide: 1⅝yd (1.40m)
                  54″ (140cm) wide: ¾yd (0.70m)
Notions: 4yd (3.60m) cord or elastic, 26″ (65cm) per casing

Sewing instructions:
Follow the instructions for model 2. The only variation is in step 3.
3 On the upper edge cut out 2¼″ (6cm) extra to fold over. The remaining edges with an extra ⅜-¾″ (1-2cm) for seam allowance.

If you are putting cords in the casings, as shown in the drawing, don't leave the fold over section at the waist open on one side. Instead, stitch both side seams, leaving openings in them for the casings as indicated on the pattern. Thread cord through the back and front casings.

CULOTTES   Model 4   173

Pattern pieces: front panel, back panel
Fabric needed: 36″ (90cm) wide: 1½yd (1.30m)
                  54″ (140cm) wide: 1½yd (1.30m)

Sewing instructions:
Follow the instructions for model 1. The only variation is in step 3 and step 11 is omitted.
3 Cut out 3″ (8cm) extra on the upper edge to fold over. The remaining edges need an extra ⅜-¾″ (1-2cm) for seam allowance.

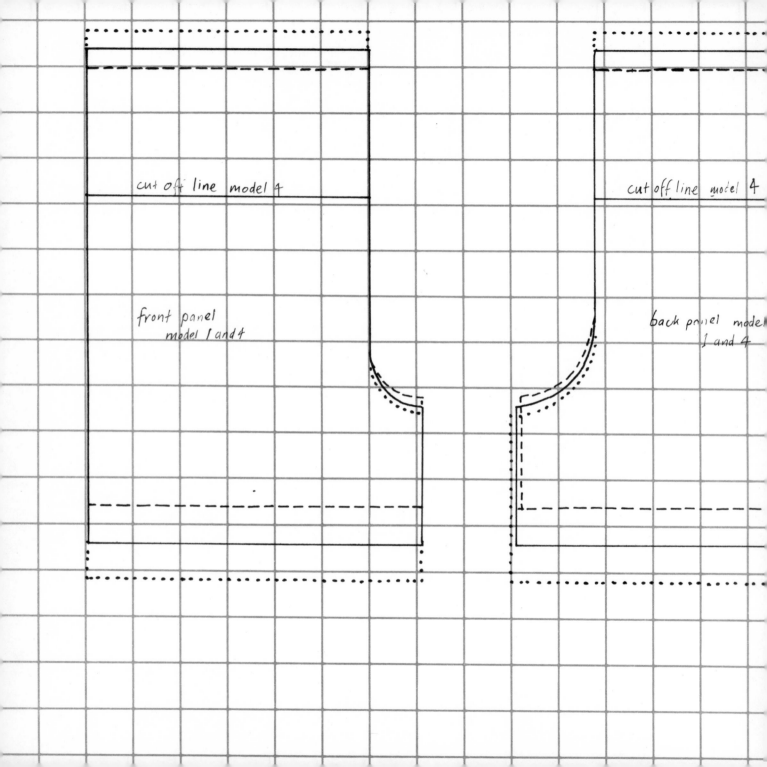

cut off line model 4

cut off line model 4

front panel
    model 1 and 4

back panel model
        1 and 4

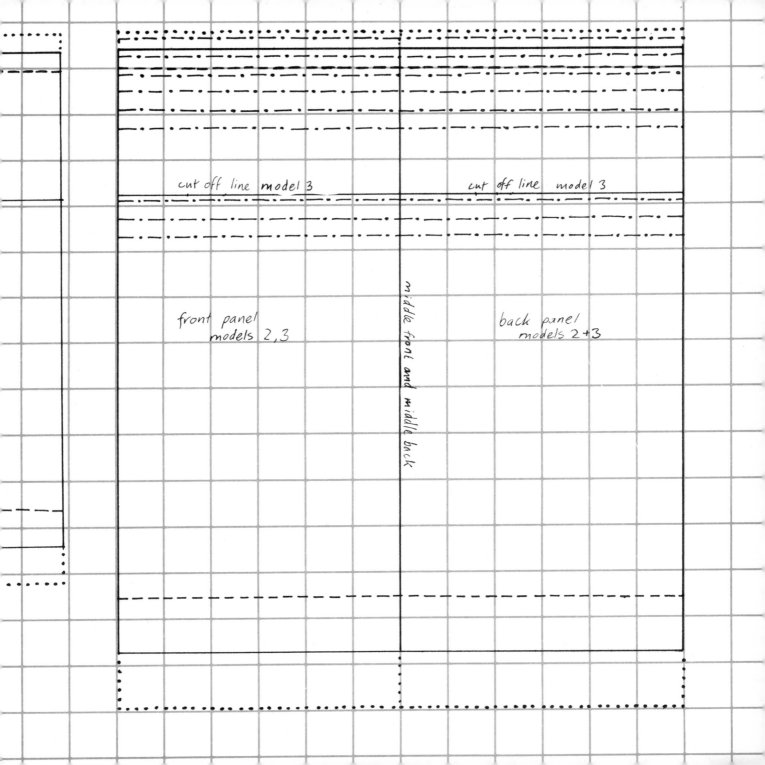

cut off line model 3   cut off line model 3

front panel
models 2,3

middle front and middle back

back panel
models 2+3

Sec P 180

Hats, Scarves, Hoods, Mittens and Bootees

Fabrics: *Remnants of woollen yarn, scraps of material.*
Printed cotton, flannel, quilted cotton, bouclé.
Lining fabric: acrylic fur, thick flannel.

SKI HAT AND SCARF   Model 1 and 6

Hat

1 Using remnants of woollen yarn knit in ribstitch (knit one, purl one) a square 8″ (20cm) wide and 8½″ (22cm) long for sizes 24″ (62cm), 27″ (68cm) and 29″ (74cm)
   8¼″ (21cm) wide and 9″ (23cm) long for sizes 32″ (80cm), 34″ (86cm) and 36″ (92cm).
   8½″ (22cm) wide and 9½″ (24cm) long for sizes 38″ (98cm), 40″ (104cm) and 42″ (110cm).
   9″ (23cm) wide and 9¾″ (25cm) long for sizes 46″ (116cm) and 48″ (122cm).
2 Sew the seam together.
3 For model 1 make two pompoms. For model 6 make one pompom (see p13 for instructions). You will need to crochet or buy a length of cord for model 1.
4 For model 1 weave the cord through the hat 1¼″ (3cm) from the top and then gather the hat together with the cord. Knot the cord and attach the pompoms to each end of the cord.
   For model 6, gather the top of the hat together and sew it. Sew the pompom on to the top.

Scarf

1 Using remnants of wool knit a strip 5½″ (14cm) wide and 42″ (110cm) long in knit one, purl one rib.
2 Sew pompoms or a fringe on to the ends.

HOODED SCARF   Model 2

1 Following the instructions, knit a scarf and knit the back part of the hood to match the pattern pieces. Mark the middle of the back part and pin this to the middle of the top edge of the scarf. Sew the back part of the hood to the edge of the scarf.
2 Sew pompoms on to the ends of the scarf (see instructions for pompoms on p13.)

BONNET   Model 3

Size by age: *0-3 mths, 9-12 mths, 3 yrs, 7 yrs*
Height of child: *24″ (62cm), 31″ (80cm), 38″ (98cm), 47″ (122cm)*

Pattern pieces: one only
Fabric needed: Taken across the width: 36″ (90cm) and 54″ (140cm) wide: ¼yd (0.25m)
   Taken along the length: 36″ (90cm) and 54″ (140cm): ¾yd (0.60m)
Lining fabric: same amount
Notions: 1⅛yd (1.0m) cord

Sewing instructions.

1 Reproduce the pattern pieces on 2 x 2″ (5 x 5cm) dressmaker's pattern paper. Mark the position of the casing and plan for seam allowance.
2 With right sides together fold the fabric in half and pin the piece to it, having the upper edge against the fabric fold.
3 Cut out with an extra ⅜-¾″ (1-2cm) for seam allowance.
4 Repeat steps 2 and 3 with lining fabric.
5 Zigzag around the edges of the pieces.

6 Stitch the middle back seam together.

7 Stitch the middle back seam of the lining fabric.

8 With the right sides together stitch both bonnets together at the front. Leave openings for the casing. Cut off the corners diagonally. Turn the right side out. Iron the bonnet flat.

9 Turn in the seam allowance on the bottom edge of both fabrics and stitch both fabrics together. At the same time, stitch around the front but leave the openings of the casing open.

10 Stitch both fabrics together where indicated on the pattern, to form the casing.

11 Thread cord through the casing.

12 Make a pompom and sew this on top of the point. (see instructions for pompoms on p13.)

BONNET WITH POMPOMS

Model 4

Size by age: *6 mths-2 yrs, 2-3½ yrs, 3½-5 yrs*

Pattern pieces: side panel, middle panel
Fabric needed: 36" (90cm) wide: ⅞yd (0.30m)
54" (140cm) wide: ¼yd (0.25m)
Lining fabric: 36" (90cm) wide: ⅞yd (0.30m)
54" (140cm) wide: ¼yd (0.25m)
Notions: 1⅛yd (1.0m) bias binding, yarn for pompoms

Sewing instructions:

1 Reproduce the pattern pieces on 2 x 2" (5 x 5cm) dressmaker's pattern paper.

2 With right sides together fold the fabric in half and pin the pieces to it, having the middle panel against the fabric fold.

179

3 Cut out the lower edge without a seam allowance, the remaining edges with an extra ⅜-¾" (1-2cm) for seam allowance.

4 Repeat steps 2 and 3 with lining fabric.

5 Zigzag around the edges of the pieces.

6 Stitch the side panels to the middle panel. Clip the seam allowance and press the seams open.

7 Repeat step 6 with lining fabric.

8 With the right sides together place both bonnets inside each other and stitch the front together. Clip the seam allowance. Turn right side out and iron the bonnet flat.

9 Topstitch through both bonnets along the seamlines and around the front.

10 Stitch bias binding around the bottom edge. Allow 28" (70cm) more bias binding than you need for the bottom edge of the bonnet and leave 14" (35cm) loose on each side of the opening.

11 Make two pompoms (see the instructions for making pompoms on p13) and sew a pompom on to the end of each tie.

HOODED SCARF

Model 5

Size by age: *0-3 mths, 9-12 mths, 3 yrs, 7 yrs*
Height of child: *24" (62cm), 31" (80cm), 38" (98cm), 47" (122cm)*

Pattern pieces: one only
Fabric needed: Taken lengthwise: 36" (90cm) and 54" (140cm) wide: 1⅞yd (1.70m)
Taken across the width: 36" (90cm) and 54" (140cm) wide: ½yd (0.50m)
Lining fabric: same amount
Notions: yarn for pompoms

Sewing instructions:

1 Reproduce the pattern piece on 2 x 2" (5 x 5cm) dressmaker's pattern paper. Remember to plan for seam allowance.
2 With right sides together fold the fabric in half and pin the pieces to it, having the upper edge against the fabric fold.
3 Cut out with an extra ⅜-¾" (1-2cm) for seam allowance.
4 Repeat steps 2 and 3 with lining fabric.
5 Zigzag around the edges of the pieces.
6 Stitch the back seam of the hood. Cut off the corner at the top diagonally.
7 Stitch the back seam on the lining fabric hood. Cut off the corner at the top diagonally.
8 With right sides together fit the hoods into each other and stitch together around the edges. Leave the lower edge open on one side in order to turn inside out. Cut off all the corners diagonally and clip the seam allowance on the neckline. Turn right side out. Press the seams flat.
9 Turn in the bottom edge that is still open, and stitch the outer fabric and the lining fabric together.
10 Make three pompoms (see the instructions for pompoms on p13) and sew them to the point of the hood and the two ends of the scarf.

BOOTEES ~~See p 185 & P 176~~ *Model 7*

Size: 6-7" (16-17cm), 7-8" (18-19cm), 8-9" (20-21cm)

Pattern pieces: sole, in-between section, upper foot
Fabric needed: 36" (90cm) wide: ¼yd (0.25m)
54" (140cm) wide: ¼yd (0.25m)
Notions: 1⅛yd (1m) bias binding

Sewing instructions:

1 Trace the pattern pieces on to transparent paper. Mark the middle on the sole. Also mark the position where the tapes are to be attached.
2 With right sides together fold the fabric in half and pin the pieces to it. The strip of fabric which comes between the sole and the upper foot is placed against the fabric fold.
3 Cut out the upper foot without a seam allowance, the remaining edges with an extra ⅜" (1cm) for seam allowance.
4 Zigzag around the edges of the pieces.
5 Stitch the middle back seam of the in-between strip. Press the seam open.
6 Stitch the middle front of the upper foot, clip the curve in the seam allowance. Press the seam open.
7 Stitch the middle back seam of the upper foot and iron the seam open. At the same time, stitch on two lengths of bias binding, each measuring 14" (35cm), where indicated on the pattern. Before stitching in place, fold each length of bias binding in half and stitch around the edges.
8 Stitch the sole to the in-between strip. Press the seam.
9 Stitch the upper foot to the in-between strip. Be sure that the middle front of the upper foot is above the middle front of the sole. The same applies to the middle back.
10 Stitch a bias binding border around the top edge.

You can also line the bootees. Just follow the instructions omitting the ties. Fit the lining bootee into the outside bootee and then stitch a bias binding border around both top edges at the same time.

MITTENS

Size by age: 3-6 months, 9-12 months, 2 years
                3 years, 5 years, 7 years

Pattern pieces: one piece. Both patterns can be
                  made with or without knitted cuffs.
Fabric needed: 36" (90cm) wide: 8 or 10" (0.20 or
                  0.25m)
                  54" (140cm) wide: 8 or 10" (0.20 or
                  0.25m)
Notions: models 1 & 2: 10" (25cm) elastic per
                  casing
                  models 3 & 4: knitted cuffs or yarn to
                  knit cuffs.

Sewing instructions Models 1 and 2:

1 Trace the mitten on to transparent paper.
2 With right sides together fold the fabric in half and
   pin the pieces to it. Remember to plan for seam
   allowance.
3 Cut out with an extra ⅜" (1cm) for seam allowance.
4 Repeat steps 2 and 3 with lining fabric.
5 Zigzag around the edges of the pieces.
6 Stitch the mittens together, leaving the bottom
   edge open. Clip the seam allowance and press the
   seam.
7 Stitch the lining fabric mittens together. Leave the
   side of the cuff open on one side. Clip the seam
   allowance and press the seam.
8 With wrong sides together, fit the mittens into each
   other. Fold in the bottom edge of both fabrics and
   stitch them together at ¼" (0.5cm) from the bottom
   edge. If desired, stitch on a cord to thread through
   the coat sleeves.

9 Stitch the casings all the way around the cuffs. The
   number of casings is optional. Thread elastic
   through the casings. Stitch the two ends of elastic
   together and then stitch up the opening.

Sewing instructions Model 3:

1 Trace the mitten on to transparent paper.
2 With right sides together fold the fabric in half and
   pin the pieces to it.
3 Cut all around without a seam allowance.
4 Zigzag around the edges of the piece.
5 Crochet all the way around the edges to join the
   mittens together.
6 Knit or buy cuffs and stitch these to the ends.

If desired, line the mitten with an inside mitten made
of lining fabric.

Sewing instructions Model 4:

1 Trace the mitten on to transparent paper.
2 With right sides together fold the fabric in half and
   pin the pieces to it. Remember to plan for seam
   allowance.
3 Cut out with an extra ¼" (0.5cm) for seam allowance all the way around.
4 Join both sections together by stitching bias binding all around the edge.
5 Knit or buy cuffs and stitch these to the ends.

If desired, line the mitten with an inside mitten made
of lining fabric.

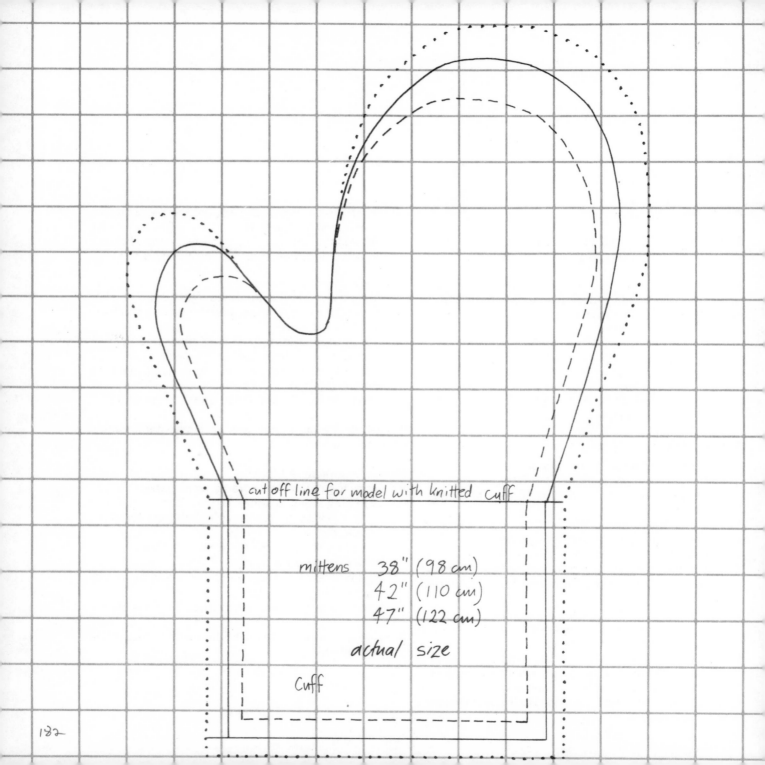

cut off line for model with knitted cuff

mittens   38" (98 cm)
           42" (110 cm)
           47" (122 cm)

actual size

Cuff

182

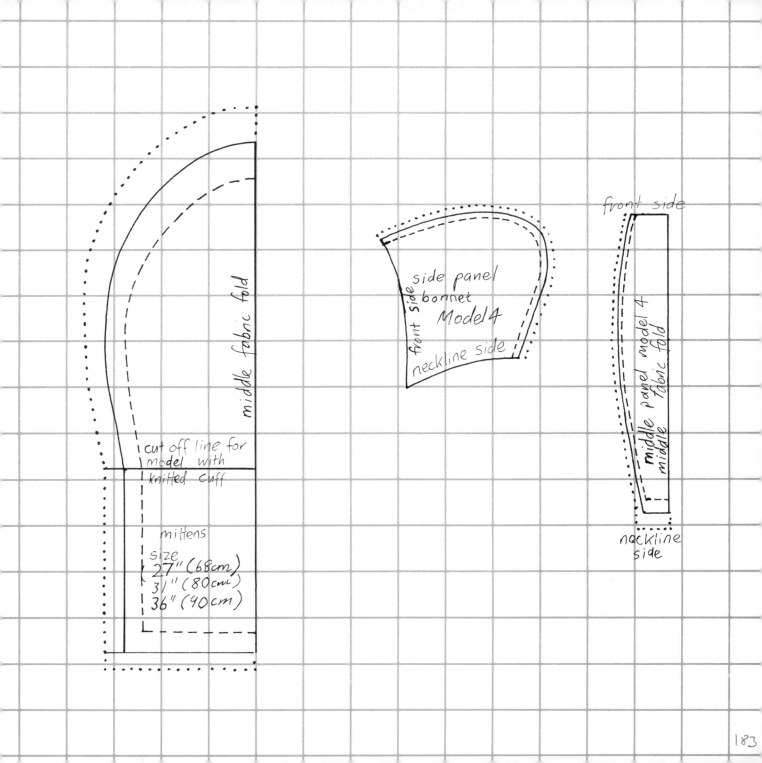

middle fabric fold

cut off line for
model with
knitted cuff

mittens

size
27" (68cm)
31" (80cm)
36" (90cm)

side panel
bonnet
Model 4

front side

neckline side

front side

front side

middle panel model 4
middle fabric fold

neckline
side

183

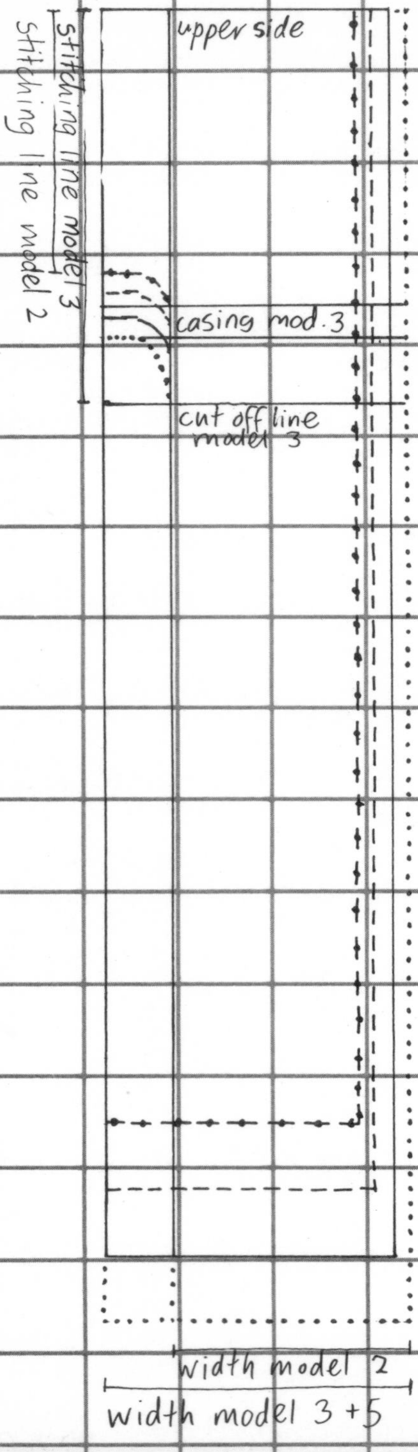

upper side

Stitching line model 3
Stitching line model 2

casing mod. 3

cut off line
model 3

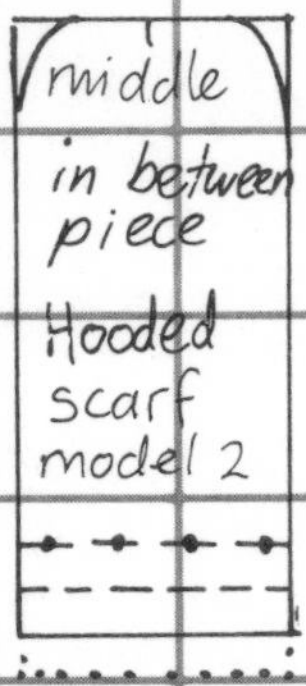

middle
in between
piece

Hooded
scarf
model 2

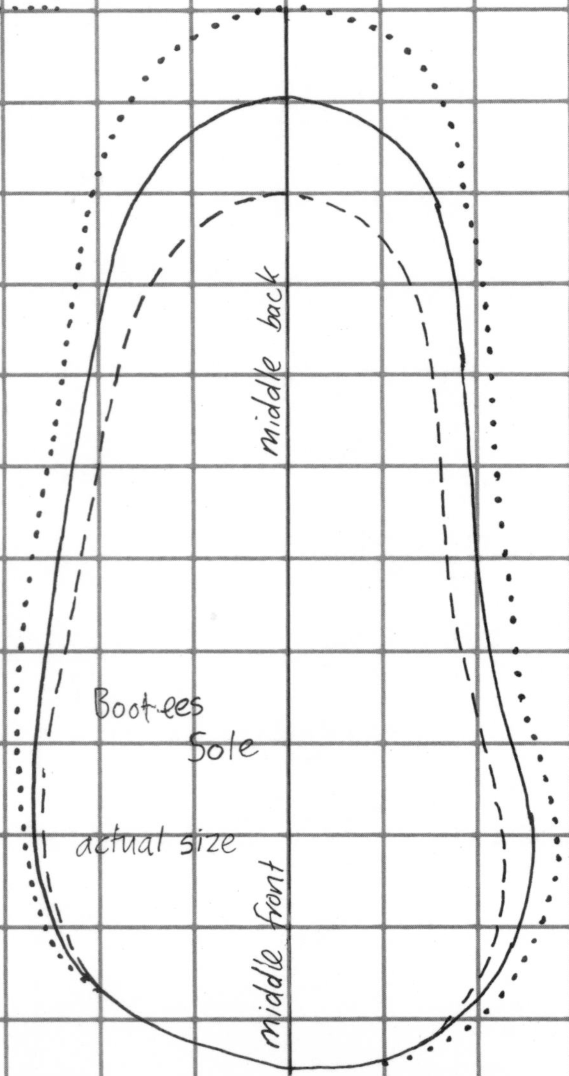

middle back

Bootees
Sole

actual size

middle front

width model 2
width model 3 + 5

184

middle front fabric fold

in between strip actual size

upper edge

Bootees
upper foot actual size

middle front

middle front

middle back

position for attaching tapes

Long 184 x?
185 x

see
P180 e P176

185

187

Bathrobe, jackets and pants

Size by age: *6-9 months, 18 months, 3 years*
Height of child: *29" (74cm), 34" (86cm), 38" (98cm)*
Fabrics: *Terrycloth, cotton, poplin, twill, jacquard, glazed cotton, corduroy, needlecord.*
Lining fabrics: flannel, tricot, terrycloth

BATHROBE AND JACKET   *Model 1 and 2*

Pattern pieces: front panel, back panel, casing, hood or collar
Fabric needed: model 1:54"(140cm)wide:1⅝yd(1.45m)
model 2:54"(140cm)wide:1¼yd (1.05m)
Lining fabric: model 1:54"(140cm)wide:1⅝yd(1.45m)
model 2:54"(140cm)wide:1¼yd(1.05m)
Notions: 1½yd (1.40m) cord, open-ended separating zipper, measure length according to pattern you are using

Sewing instructions:

1. Reproduce the pattern pieces on 2 x 2" (5 x 5cm) dressmaker's pattern paper. Remember to plan for seam allowance. Mark the position of the casing on the pattern.
2. With right sides together fold the fabric in half and pin the pieces to it, having the middle of the back, the casing and in model 2 the collar, placed against the fabric fold.
3. Cut out the middle front with an extra ¾" (2cm) for seam allowance. Allow an extra ⅜-¾" (1-2cm) on the remaining edges for seam allowance.
4. Now fold the lining fabric in half and pin the pieces to it, having the middle of the back against the fabric fold. Leave out the pattern for casing.
Cut out the pieces as described in step 3.

5. Zigzag around the edges of the pieces.
6. Stitch the upper arm seams and the underarm side seams together. Clip the curves in the seam allowance and press the seams open.
7. Stitch the upper arm seams and the underarm side seams of the lining fabric together. Clip the curve in the seam allowance and press the seams open.
8. Stitch the hood sections together (this does not apply to model 2). Clip the curve in the seam allowance and press the seam open.
9. Stitch the hood sections of the lining fabric together (this does not apply to model 2). Clip the seam allowance and press the seam open.
10. Stitch the hood or the collar to the neckline. Clip the seam allowance and press the seam open.
11. Stitch the hood or collar lining to the neckline of the garment lining. Clip the seam allowance and press the seam open.
12. With right sides together, fit the lining into the garment. Stitch the bottom edge of the sleeves together. Stitch the front edge of the hood or the top edge of the collar together. Clip the curve in the seam allowance.
13. Turn the garment right side out and iron the seams flat.
14. Turn in and iron the seam allowance of the middle front. Do the same with the lining fabric. Baste the zipper in between both fabrics and stitch in place. Continue stitching to the bottom edge of the garment. (See p14 for how to insert zipper.)
15. Turn in the seam allowance of the casing all the way around and stitch it on through both thicknesses as indicated on the pattern.
16. Turn in the hemline of both fabrics and stitch both fabrics together along the edge of the garment.

17 Top-stitch along the front edge of the hood or the top edge of the collar.
18 Topstitch around the bottom edge of the sleeves.
19 Thread the cord through the casing.

JACKET WITH OR WITHOUT HOOD   *Model 3 and 4*

Pattern pieces: front panel, back panel, collar or hood
Fabric needed: model3:54"(140cm)wide:1¼yd(1.05m)
                    model4:54"(140cm)wide:1⅜yd (1.20m)
Lining fabric: model3: 54"(140cm)wide:1¼yd(1.05m)
                    model4:54"(140cm)wide:1⅜yd(1.20m)
Notions: 1½yd (1.40m) cord, open-ended separating zipper

Sewing instructions:
1 Reproduce the pattern pieces on 2 x 2" (5 x 5cm) dressmaker's pattern paper. Remember to plan for seam allowance.
2 With right sides together fold the fabric in half and pin the pieces to it, having the middle of the back and collar (if applicable) against the fabric fold.
3 The middle of the front is cut out with an extra ¾" (2cm) for seam allowance. Cut out the lower edge of the sleeves and the lower edge of the jacket with an extra 1¼" (3cm) for seam allowance. Allow an extra ⅜-¾" (1-2cm) for seam allowance on the remaining edges.
4 Now fold the lining fabric in half and pin the pieces to it, having the middle of the back and collar (if applicable) against the fabric fold. Cut out the pieces as described in step 3.
5 Zigzag around the edges of the pieces.
6 Stitch the upper arm seams and the underarm side seams. Clip the curves in the seam allowance and press the seams open.

189

7 Stitch the upper arm seams and the underarm side seams of the lining fabric together. Clip the curve in the seam allowance and press the seams open.
8 Stitch the hood sections together (this does not apply to model 3). Clip the curve in the seam allowance and press the seams open.
9 Stitch the hood lining sections together (this does not apply to model 3). Clip the seam allowance and press the seam open.
10 Stitch the collar or the hood to the neckline. Clip the seam allowance and press the seam open.
11 Stitch the hood or collar lining to the neckline of the jacket lining. Clip the seam allowance and press the seam open.
12 With right sides together, fit both jackets into each other. Stitch the fronts of the hoods or the tops of the collars together. Clip the seam allowance. Stitch the bottom edges of the sleeves together, leaving a small opening for the elastic.
13 Turn the jacket right side out. Iron the seams flat.
14 Turn in and iron the seam allowance on the middle front. Do the same with the lining fabric. Baste the zipper in between both fabrics and stitch in place, stopping 1¼" (3cm) from the hemline. Leave this section open. (See p14 for how to insert zipper.)
15 Top-stitch around the front edge of the hood or the top edge of the collar.
16 Fold in ⅜" (1cm) along the hemline of both fabrics and stitch both fabrics together, close to the bottom edge.
17 Do another row of stitching ⅝" (1.5cm) from the first row.
18 Thread the cord through the casing.

PANTS

Pattern pieces: pants front, pants back
Fabric needed: 36" (90cm) wide: 1¾yd (1.60m)
54" (140cm) wide: ⅞yd (0.80m)
for the short pants:
36" (90cm) wide: ⅞yd (0.80m)
54" (140cm) wide: ½yd (0.40m)
Notions: 24" (60cm) elastic ⅜" (1cm) wide
43" (110cm) elastic for baggy pants

Sewing instructions:

1 Reproduce the pattern pieces on 2 x 2" (5 x 5cm) dressmaker's pattern paper. Remember to plan for seam allowance.
2 With right sides together fold the fabric in half and pin the pieces to it.
3 Allow an extra 1" (2.5cm) for seam allowance at the top and the bottom. If making baggy pants, allow an extra 2¾" (7cm) for seam allowance at the bottom edge.
Cut the remaining edges with an extra ⅜-¾" (1-2cm) for seam allowance.
4 Zigzag around the edges of the pieces.
5 Stitch the inside leg seams of the front and back together. Press the seams open.
6 Stitch the crotch seams together. Stitch the front panels together and the back panels together. Clip the curves in the seam allowance. Press the seams open.
7 Stitch the side seams together. Press the seams open.
8 Turn in 1" (2.5cm) along the bottom edge of the legs and stitch around ⅝" (1.5cm) from the bottom edge. In the case of baggy pants, leave a small opening in order to insert the elastic. Stitch the two ends of elastic together, and stitch up the opening.
9 Turn in 1" (2.5cm) along the upper edge of the pants. Stitch around ⅝" (1.5cm) from the upper edge. Leave a small opening. Insert the elastic. Stitch both ends of the elastic together and stitch up the opening.

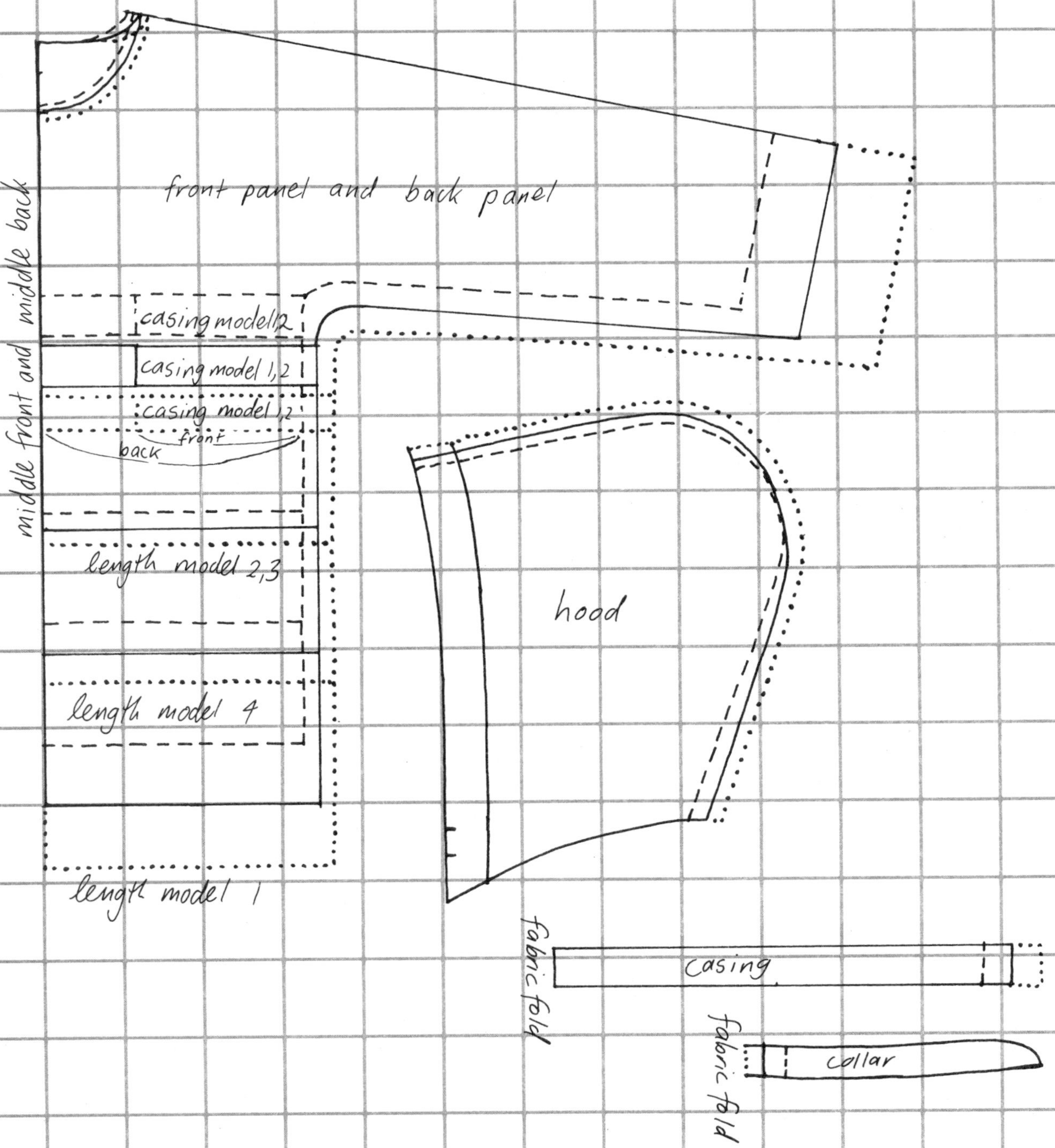

front panel and back panel

middle back

middle front and middle back

casing model 2

casing model 1,2

casing model 1,2

front

back

length model 2,3

length model 4

length model 1

hood

fabric fold

casing

fabric fold

collar

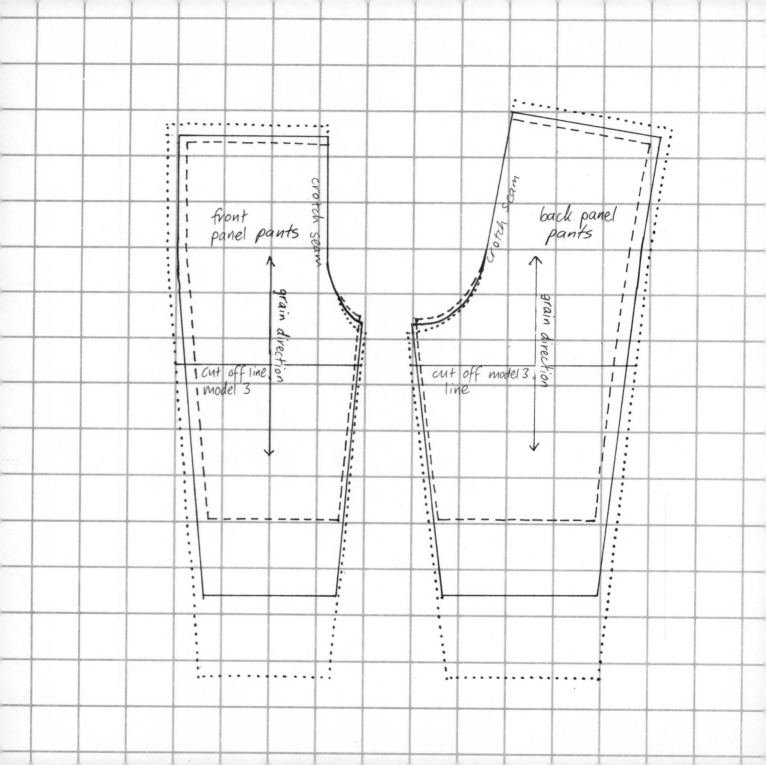

front
panel pants

crotch seam

grain direction

Cut off line
model 3

back panel
pants

crotch seam

grain direction

cut off model 3
line

1   2

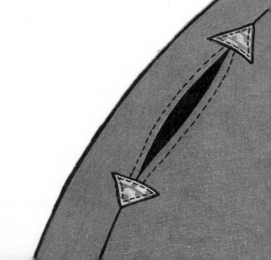

Poncho, knitted pullover and cape

Size by age: *6-9 mths, 18 mths, 3 yrs, 5 yrs, 7 yrs*
Height of child: *29" (74cm), 34" (86cm), 38" (98cm), 43" (110cm), 47" (122cm)*
Fabrics: *Oilcloth, twill, gabardine, corduroy, needlecord*

PONCHO
Model 1

Pattern pieces: front panel, back panel, hood, hood facing
Fabric needed: 48" (120cm) wide: 1⅞yd (1.70m)
54" (140cm) wide: 1⅞yd (1.70m)
Notions: 8" (20cm) zipper, snap fasteners, bias binding

Sewing instructions:

1 Reproduce the pattern pieces on 2 x 2" (5 x 5cm) dressmaker's pattern paper. Remember to plan for seam allowance.
2 With right sides together fold the fabric in half and pin the pattern to it, having the middle of the back against the fabric fold.
3 Cut out the side and the bottom edge without a seam allowance. Allow an extra ¾" (2cm) on the middle front for seam allowance and an extra ⅜-¾" (1-2cm) on the remaining edges.
4 Zigzag around the edges of the pieces.
5 Stitch the middle front seam, stopping 8" (20cm) from the neckline. Press the seam open.
6 Stitch the shoulder seams and press them open.
7 Stitch the hood sections together. Clip the curve in the seam allowance and press the seam open.
8 Stitch the hood facings together at the top. Press the seam open.

9 With right sides together stitch the hood facing to the right side of the hood. If you wish, leave a small opening where indicated on the pattern in order to insert a cord. Clip the seam allowance. Turn in the facing and iron the seam flat.
10 Turn the facing out again and then stitch the hood to the neckline. Clip the seam allowance and press the seam open.
11 Stitch the zipper into the middle front seam. (See p14 for how to insert zipper.)
12 Turn the facing back in and topstitch ¾" (2cm) from the outer edge.
13 Finish the edges of the poncho with bias binding.
14 Attach snap fasteners where indicated.

KNITTED PULLOVER
Model 2

Pattern pieces: front panel, back panel
Notions: knitting yarn and knitting needles

Instructions:
1 Reproduce the pattern pieces on 2 x 2" (5 x 5cm) dressmaker's pattern paper.
2 Fold a piece of paper in half and pin the pattern to it, having the middle of the front, middle of the back against the fabric fold. Cut the pieces out around the pattern.
3 Knit a front panel and a back panel to match the pieces in a plain stitch.
4 Sew the upper arm seams together. Leave 8" (20cm) open for the neckline.
5 Sew the underarm side seams together.
6 Finish off the upper and lower seams with a decorative stitch.

You can also use this pattern to make a new top for the baby from an old full-sized pullover or T-shirt.

Sewing instructions:
1 Follow steps 1 and 2 for the knitted pullover.
2 Place the pattern pieces on the pullover or T-shirt. Cut out the pieces with an extra ⅜-¾″ (1-2cm) for seam allowance.
3 Zigzag around the edges of the pieces.
4 Using a small zigzag stitch, stitch the shoulder seams as far as the mark, and also stitch the side and underarm seams.
5 Stitch the neckline and hemline by hand.

If the pattern piece is too large for the pullover then you can cut off the whole sleeve, or part of it, from the pattern. This part is then cut out of the sleeve of the pullover. Zigzag around the edge and sew it on to the garment.

CAPE   *Model 3*

Pattern pieces: front panel, back panel, hood, hood facing
Fabric required: 48″ (120cm) wide: 1⅞yd (1.70m)
54″ (140cm) wide: 1⅞yd (1.70m)
Notions: 8″ (20cm) zipper

Sewing instructions:
1 Reproduce the pattern pieces on 2 x 2″ (5 x 5cm) dressmaker's pattern paper. Remember to plan for seam allowance.
2 With right sides together fold the fabric in half and pin the pieces to it, having the middle of the back against the fabric fold.

3 Cut out the middle front with an extra ¾″ (2cm) for seam allowance. Allow an extra ⅜-¾″ (1-2cm) on the remaining edges for seam allowance.
4 Zigzag around the edges of the pieces.
5 Stitch the middle front seam, stopping 8″ (20cm) from the neckline. Press the seam open.
6 Stitch the side seams, leaving an opening where indicated. Clip the curves in the seam allowance of the side seams. Press the seams open.

Follow steps 7, 8, 9, 10, 11 and 12 for poncho.

13 Turn in ⅜″ (1cm) along the hemline of the cape and stitch it.
14 If desired, cut out 4 triangles. Turn in ¼″ (0.5cm) all the way around and stitch these on to the ends of the openings for the hands. This will prevent the seams tearing open.

knitted pullover
model 2

middle front and middle back

opening for hands

Cape model 3

middle front and middle back

Zipper

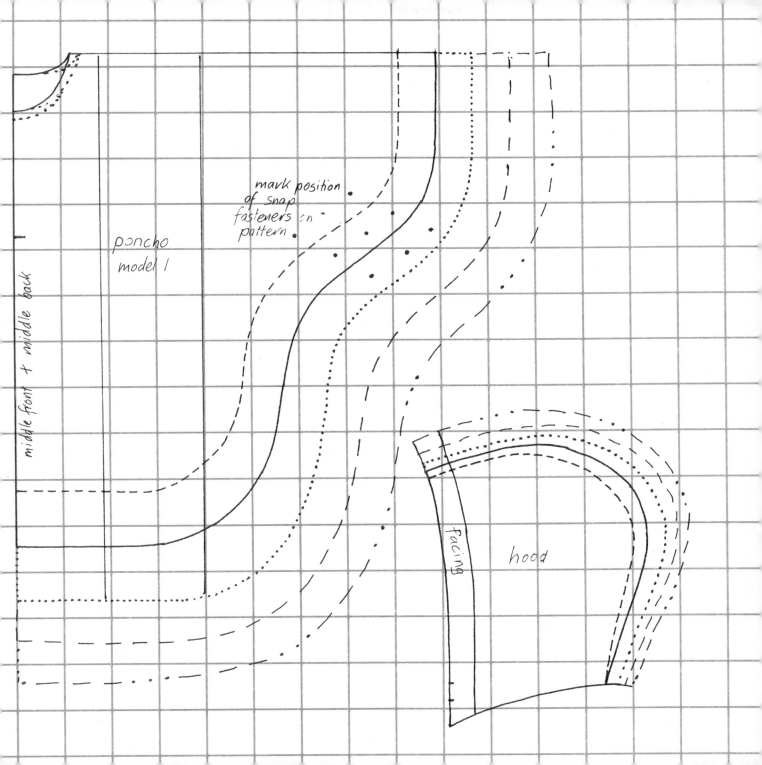

mark position
of snap
fasteners on
pattern

poncho
model 1

middle front + middle back

facing

hood

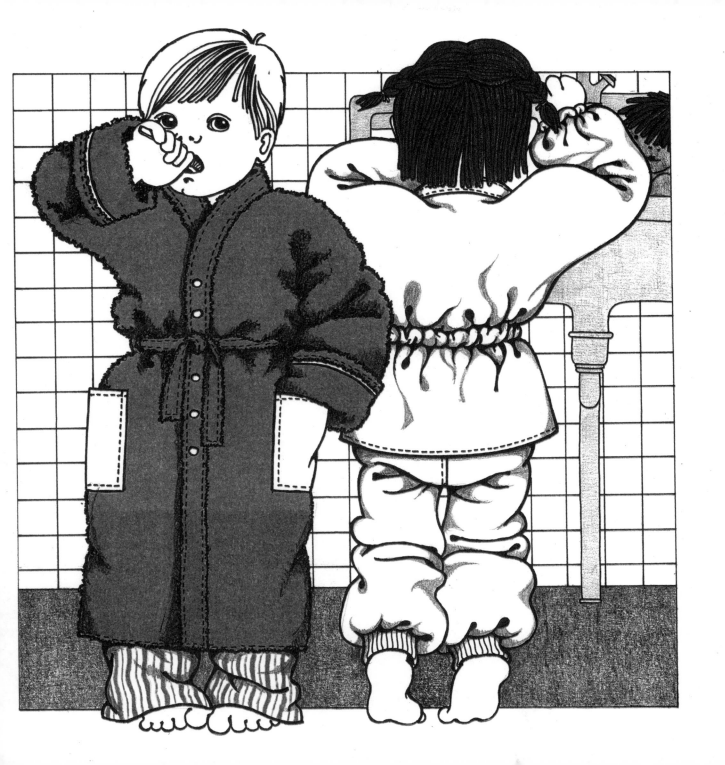

Bathrobe, nightclothes and jackets

Size by age: *2 years,   4 years,   6 years*
Height of child: *38" (92cm), 40" (104cm), 45" (116cm)*
Fabrics: *For the bathrobe: terrycloth or flannel*
for the nightclothes: tricot or terrycloth
for the jackets: twill, bouclé, corduroy,
gabardine lined with acrylic fur,
corduroy lined with flannel.

BATHROBE   Model 1

Pattern pieces: front panel, back panel, collar border, pocket, tie belt
Fabric needed: 54" (140cm) wide: 2⅝yd (2.40m)
Notions: ¾yd (70cm) bias binding or ribbon, snap fasteners, fabric remnant for the pockets, 1⅛yd (1.0m) iron-on interfacing

Sewing instructions:

1. Reproduce the pattern pieces on 2 x 2" (5 x 5cm) dressmaker's pattern paper. Mark the position of the pocket and plan for seam allowance.
2. With right sides together fold the fabric in half and pin the pieces to it, having the middle back and the tie belt against the fabric fold. Cut out the collar border twice, the second one is the facing.
3. Cut out the lower edge of the sleeves with an extra 1½" (4cm) for seam allowance. The hemline of the front and back panels, the bottom edge of the collar border and its facing are all cut out with an extra 1" (2.5cm) for seam allowance. The remaining edges with an extra ⅜-¾" (1-2cm).
4. Zigzag around the edges of the pieces.
5. Stitch the underarm side seams. Clip the curve in the seam allowance and press the seams open. If the pockets are to be stitched in with the side seams, see step 6 before you start stitching.
6. Turn in and iron the seam allowance around the pockets. Turn in and stitch the upper edge. Stitch the pockets on where indicated on the front panels adjacent to the side seams. If you wish you can stitch one side of each pocket in with the side seams. In that case that side of the pocket need not be turned in and stitched on to the fabric.
7. Stitch the upper arm seams and press them open.
8. Stitch the middle back seam of the collar border and press it open.
9. Stitch the border all the way around the front and the neckline. Clip the curve in the seam allowance.
10. Iron the interfacing on to the wrong side of the front collar border facing.
11. With right sides together stitch the facing to the border. Clip curves in the seam allowance. Turn the border and facing with the right sides out. Iron the border flat.
12. Turn in and iron all the seam allowances on the collar border facing.
13. Fold in the bottom edge and stitch ¾" (2cm) from the edge.
14. Stitch around the facing of the collar border close to the seam. Stitch again around the outer edge.
15. Turn in ¼" (0.5cm) along the bottom edge of the sleeves and then repeat folding ¾" (2cm) in. Pin ribbon or bias binding under the fold so that part of the ribbon is showing. Stitch along the ribbon and seam at the same time. Turn out 1½" (4cm) around the sleeves to form a cuff.
16. Attach snap fasteners to the front border.
17. Turn in and press the seam allowance all around the tie belt. Fold the tie belt in half and iron it. Stitch it all the way around, keeping close to the edges.

NIGHTCLOTHES – TOP

Model 2

Pattern pieces: front panel, back panel, collar border, pocket (optional)
Fabric needed: 54″ (140cm) wide: 2yd (1.75m)
Notions: 24″ (60cm) ruched lingerie elastic ¾″ (2cm) wide or wider

Sewing instructions:

Follow the instructions for model 1. Cut out the length as indicated on the pattern. Mark the position of the elastic on the front and back panel.
There are variations in steps 5 and 15, and step 17 is omitted.

5 Once the underarm side seams are stitched together as in step 5, the ruched lingerie elastic can be stitched where indicated on the pattern.

15 Fold in 1″ (2.5cm) along the bottom edges of the sleeves and stitch ⅝″ (1.5cm) from the bottom edge. Leave a small opening for the elastic. Thread the elastic through the casing. Stitch the two ends of elastic together and then stitch up the opening.

NIGHTCLOTHES – BOTTOM

Pattern pieces: front panel, back panel
Fabric needed: 54″ (140cm) wide: 1yd (0.85m)
Notions: knitted cuffs for the ends of the legs

Sewing instructions:

Follow the instructions for the overalls on page 118, model 3. Omit all references to the bib. Cut along the ends of the legs with an extra ⅜-¾″ (1-2cm) for seam allowance and attach knitted cuffs to the ends.

JACKET WITH POCKETS

Model 3

Pattern pieces: front panel, back panel, collar border, pocket
Fabric needed: 54″ (140cm) wide: 2yd (1.75m)
Notions: 1⅛yd (1.0m) twill tape or any strong cotton tape ¾″ (2cm) wide, 8 D-rings

Sewing instructions:

Follow the instructions for model 1. Cut out length as indicated on the pattern.
There are variations in steps 9 and 15; steps 16 and 17 are omitted.

9 Stitch the collar border all the way around along the front panels. At the same time stitch on four loops of tape on one side. First slide two D-rings on to each loop. On the other side, stitch on four 2¾″ (7cm) lengths of tape. Fold each length in half and stitch along both edges. Before you stitch the loops and strips of tape in place, decide which front panel is to wrapover on top.

15 Fold in 1″ (2.5cm) along the bottom edge of the sleeves and stitch down ⅝″ (1.5cm) from the bottom edge. Leave a small opening. Insert the elastic. Stitch both ends of elastic together and then stitch up the opening.

JACKET WITH KNITTED CUFFS

Model 4

Pattern pieces: front panel, back panel, collar border
Fabric needed: 54″ (140cm) wide: 2yd (1.75m)
Notions: 1⅛yd (1.0m) twill tape or any strong cotton tape ⅝″ (2cm) wide, knitted cuffs for the sleeves, 28″ (70cm) ruched lingerie elastic 1⅛″ (3cm) wide, 8 D-rings

Sewing instructions:

Follow the instructions for model 1. Cut out the length as indicated on the pattern.

There are variations in steps 3, 9, 13 and 15. Steps 6, 16 and 17 are omitted.

3 All pieces are cut out with an extra ⅜-¾" (1-2cm) for seam allowance.

13 Comes between steps 7 and 8. Fold in the seam allowance on the bottom edge. Stitch ruched lingerie elastic all the way around.

9 Stitch the collar border all the way around along both front panels. At the same time, stitch on four loops of tape. First slide two D-rings on to each loop. At the same time, on the other side stitch on four 2¾" (7cm) lengths of tape. Fold each length of tape in half and stitch along both edges. Choose which panel is to wrap over on top, before you stitch on the loops and tapes.

Before stitching along the bottom edge of the collar border, turn it in so that it is level with the rest of the bottom edge of the jacket.

15 Stitch the knitted cuffs on to the sleeves.

middle back neckline

border for neckline and front panel

attachment points for tapes

Cut off line for Short model

crotch seam

front panel bottom model 2

side seam

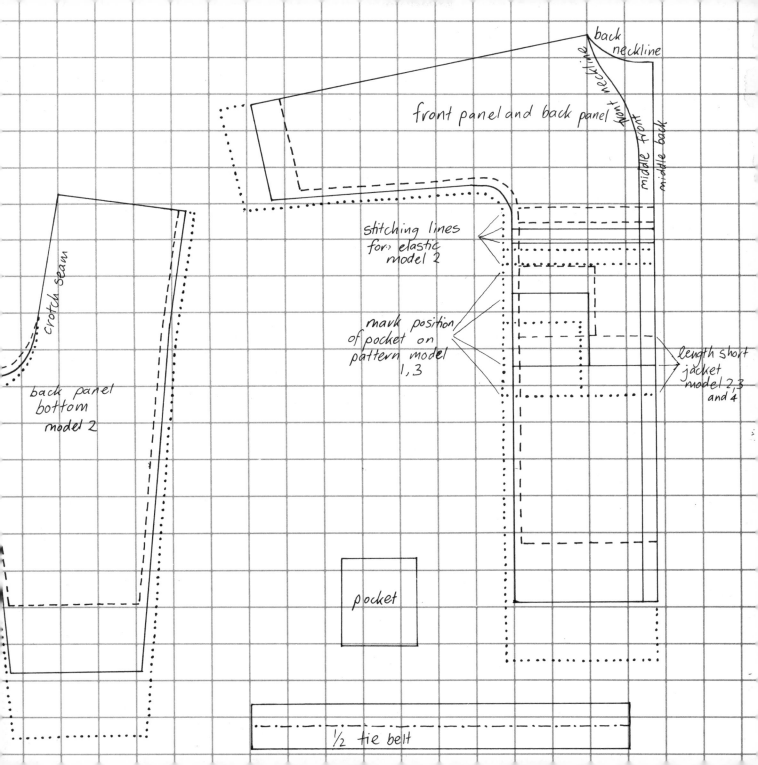

front panel and back panel

back neckline

front neckline

middle front

middle back

stitching lines for elastic model 2

mark position of pocket on pattern model 1, 3

length short jacket model 2, 3 and 4

crotch seam

back panel bottom model 2

pocket

½ tie belt